"As someone who recently experienced deep pain and hardship—and had to learn how to embrace a new journey—I find *Forty day and Forty Nights* is a comforting reminder that God is present with us, forming us, leading us, and helping us to embrace the new journey. As you read about biblical characters who faced trials and hardships, hopefully these examples will remind you that God is with you to help you embrace this new journey."

—Mark Maddix, lead pastor, San Dieguito United Methodist Church, Encinitas, California

"Many of us think the Bible's heroes are larger-than-life individuals who share little in common with us today. Allen breaks through that façade. Noah? Ezekiel? Jonah? Different contexts, same hardships. If you're a preacher like me, get ready for an avalanche of inspiration! If you work with Christians in crisis, you'll want to revisit these characters with Allen as your guide. His candid personal stories give us courage to face our own."

—Casey Banks, United Methodist Elder

"Out of the crucible of his own life, Patrick Allen writes with empathy for those of us who are in a messy season of life. His reflections, drawn from several biblical events described as forty days and forty nights in duration, are rich with wisdom and inspiration which invites us to draw on God's provision when life gets messy."

—Joe Watkins, senior pastor, First Church of the Nazarene of Pasadena

"Patrick Allen guides readers through the setbacks, doubts, and challenges of some key biblical figures, showing how God's faithfulness is revealed in life's darkest moments. This isn't a self-help book, but a journey through real struggles, urging trust in God and hope in the wilderness. Through our own forty-day trials, Allen shows how God's grace, community, and faith grow, reminding us that we're not forgotten."

—GREG APPLEBY, LEAD PASTOR, CHURCH OF THE NAZARENE, LEAVENWORTH, WASHINGTON

Forty Days and Forty Nights

Forty Days and Forty Nights

The Hardships and Transitions We Face

PATRICK ALLEN

WIPF & STOCK · Eugene, Oregon

FORTY DAYS AND FORTY NIGHTS
The Hardships and Transitions We Face

Copyright © 2024 Patrick Allen. All rights reserved. Except for brief quotations in critical publications or reviews, no part of this book may be reproduced in any manner without prior written permission from the publisher. Write: Permissions, Wipf and Stock Publishers, 199 W. 8th Ave., Suite 3, Eugene, OR 97401.

Wipf & Stock
An Imprint of Wipf and Stock Publishers
199 W. 8th Ave., Suite 3
Eugene, OR 97401

www.wipfandstock.com

PAPERBACK ISBN: 979-8-3852-3382-3
HARDCOVER ISBN: 979-8-3852-3383-0
EBOOK ISBN: 979-8-3852-3384-7

11/18/24

All Scripture quotations, unless otherwise noted, are taken from The Holy Bible New International Version NIV. Copyright, 1973, 1978, 1984, 2011 by Biblica, Inc. Used by Permission. All rights reserved worldwide.

Scripture quotations marked NRSVUE are taken from the New Revised Standard Version Updated Edition. Copyright © 2021 National Council of Churches of Christ in the United States of America. Used by permission. All rights reserved worldwide.

"For Today," a prayer found in *Forward Day by Day*, used by permission. Forward Movement, 412 Sycamore Street, Cincinnati, OH, 45202.

To Lori, who has taught me how to face the giants who taunt us and the disappointments that come our way with grace, courage, and faith. Without her example, all this would be empty words.

For me, it all comes down to this:
Life is messy, but God is faithful.

Contents

Preface | ix

Introduction: Trying Times That Come Our Way | xi

Chapter One: Setbacks—Moses | 1

Chapter Two: Giants—David | 16

Chapter Three: Floods—Noah | 33

Chapter Four: Despair—Elijah | 46

Chapter Five: Silence—Ezekiel | 59

Chapter Six: Reversals—Jonah | 77

Chapter Seven: Temptations—Jesus | 91

Chapter Eight: Disbelief—Jesus and His Followers | 101

Epilogue | 111

Preface

I THOUGHT WITH THE publication of *Practicing the Prayer of St. Francis* it might be the end of writing for publication. Honestly, I felt like I was running out of steam a bit (age has a way of doing that to you), and I didn't have anything particularly in mind. Maybe I had shared all that I knew to share—maybe even more than I knew to share. Then, I was called into a small, fiercely-lit consultation room at the local hospital to join my wife as we received a cancer diagnosis. In that instant, everything changed. Washing the car, mowing the lawn, and all the other plans of the day instantly faded away. They simply vanished. The only things that mattered were understanding the diagnosis and getting the best care possible. Much like Noah, we were faced with a flood that would change everything, but we didn't even have time to build an ark. We were at sea on a quickly assembled life raft.

And as many who have dealt with cancer will attest, it wasn't a one-and-done affair. It was a hard journey, one gut punch after another. As of this writing, however, I am happy to report that things are looking up; but the journey continues. Floods change you. They change what you believe to be important, how you see the world around you, and how you want to live your life. Floods change everything.

Ancient writers, struggling to describe times of hardship, testing, or trial as well as times of great change and transition often used metaphors in an attempt to convey the depth and trauma of such times. In the Bible, *forty days and forty nights* is one such metaphor. It conveys more than just forty calendar days, much more. Perhaps because of the flood that my wife and I experienced, I have been drawn to this metaphor in recent days. I want to explore eight instances in particular, not as a biblical scholar, not as a theologian, not as an exemplary Christian, but as one who has lived through forty days and nights. I want to offer some wisdom and comfort to those who are facing floods, giants, disappointments, reversals, temptations, despair, disbelief, even times to be silent. We know that forty days are hard, and forty nights are even harder—and longer too. My prayer is that this book will provide some insight and hope to you for your own forty days and nights, regardless of what life brings your way.

I have come to believe this: life is messy, but God is faithful. I hope you will come to believe this too.

Introduction: Trying Times That Come Our Way

IT IS ALMOST IMPOSSIBLE to read the Bible regularly without noticing the repetition of certain words and events. Clearly, numbers were important for writers in biblical times, and some carried significant spiritual symbolism that would have been recognized and understood by those who read biblical texts or heard the stories.

Perhaps the most fascinating use of numbers in the Bible is actually a phrase rather than a single number, depicting some sort of length of time: *forty days and forty nights*. It is found in the Bible over twenty times, referring to floods, taunting by giants, major setbacks, temptations, reversals, unbelief, despair, even times to be silent. We may ask, Does this phrase mean precisely forty calendar days or simply a very long time? And is it referring only to a specific length of time or is it a representation of a significant life transition? In other words, is the phrase temporal or spiritual—or both? Good questions all.

Quite frankly, I don't think it matters because the takeaways from this book are the same regardless of how literally one reads these stories. What I am attempting to do is to mine and apply a theological understanding of God and the human condition to our own lives, especially when we experience our own version of forty days and forty nights. It doesn't require a particular reading of the Bible to join in this conversation. But to be clear, I acknowledge that, in this book, forty days and forty nights is not always understood to be literal. At times it might be, but it doesn't have to be. It

INTRODUCTION: TRYING TIMES THAT COME OUR WAY

can also be a symbolic period of time, a long time, a tough time—the dark night (or nights) of the soul, if you will. It can identify and signify a significant time of hardship, trial, or difficulty, and it is often indicative of a time of transition or starting over too. Things that come to us more than we seek them out.

This book will examine eight instances of forty days and nights found in the Bible. As we will see, these types of forty days and nights come to each of us too, and sometimes more than once. We will walk with Moses as he faces three major leadership setbacks, once after meeting with God on the mountaintop, once after sending out the spies to explore the land of Canaan (both events involved forty days and nights), and once when a total leadership transition was in order, but he didn't see it coming. Many leaders don't (chapter 1). We will watch David as he prepares to fight the giant who taunted the Israelite army, including some of his brothers, for forty days and forty nights. It won't be the only giant he will face in his lifetime (chapter 2). We will examine the story of Noah and what it means to face the floods of life after forty days and nights of rain—and the challenges of starting over (chapter 3). And we will journey with Elijah as he makes a pilgrimage of forty days and nights to meet with God on Mt. Horeb. His despair was in full view like a bad haircut (chapter 4).

We will mark time with Ezekiel when God commanded him to be silent and still for forty days and nights—not the default mode for any prophet worth his salt (chapter 5). We will sit under a fast-growing plant with Jonah, who was seething and wondering what just happened when, after he finally prophesied destruction to the Ninevites in the next forty days and nights, God relented and pulled the proverbial rug out from under him. He felt, at the very least, silly and betrayed (chapter 6).

We will spend forty days and nights in a wilderness with Jesus and examine the temptations that came his way, and the temptations that come our way too (chapter 7), and end by seeing how Jesus dealt with his own followers' disbelief during the forty days and nights between his resurrection and his ascension (chapter 8). We've all struggled at one time or another with those who didn't believe in us or in the work we felt called to do—and sometimes we didn't muster much belief in ourselves either. It is as common as the flu.

Forty days and forty nights—full of hardships, trials, struggles, and disappointments, but also a time of transition, pregnant with the hope for a new beginning or a second chance. This is the stuff of life. Together we will walk with those who have gone before us, gleaning wisdom from their stories, and trusting that they will provide some lamp posts and guideposts for all of us as we face the forty days and nights that challenge us and shape us as we make our way home.

CHAPTER ONE

Setbacks—Moses

God led the people by the roundabout way of the wilderness bordering the Red Sea.

—EXOD 13:18 NRSVUE

THE ROUNDABOUT WAY OF THE WILDERNESS: A PERSONAL STORY

THIS IS A STORY about traveling on the other road. You think you're doing all the right things—exactly what God wants you to do, exactly what you feel called to do, but your plans don't work out. You find yourself traveling down another road, the roundabout way of the wilderness. Have you been there? The truth of the matter is that at some point in our lives, we've all been there—or will be. Here's my story:

When I graduated from college, all I really wanted to do was to be involved in an organized basketball program in some way—any way. Basketball was my favorite sport, a sport in which I lettered in both high school and college. Honestly, I had my heart set on trying to catch on with a professional team at some level, but a kind scout took me aside at an open tryout one afternoon and told me that that wouldn't happen. "Son," he said as he looked me straight in the eyes, "you have great desire, a strong work ethic, an accurate jump shot, a coachable attitude, and a true love for the game. That's all well and good, but you lack one basic thing—the physical ability to play at the next level." Needless to say, missing that "one basic thing" spelled the end of my dreams of playing at the next level.

I went to work for a college as the housing director on their student life staff, and worked part-time at a local bank to make ends meet. A year later, I joined the university full-time and, just before the start of basketball season, the head coach asked me if I would be interested in serving as his assistant, even though the hours were long and the pay was minimal (in fact, nonexistent). I honestly didn't care. To be working with college athletes and spending time in the gym again was truly an answer to prayer. Life was good. I was going to be a coach and I felt very close to God!

Truthfully, the team wasn't all that good, but it didn't matter. I was doing exactly what I wanted to do, exactly what I felt called to do, living life in the sweet spot. After two years together, the coach called me into his office and told me that he had accepted a coaching position in another state. He said that I could join him, but he didn't think that I would accept. He was right. I was in the middle of a graduate program and working full-time at the college as the associate dean of students. A big move just wasn't possible. Actually, he anticipated my answer and told me that he had already met with the athletic director and recommended me for the head coaching position. He advised me to meet with the AD some time over the next week or two. I was sitting in his office in less than twenty minutes! It was all so exciting.

The AD told me that he had been watching me for the past two years, and he felt that I was ready for the assignment. However, since I worked on the student life staff and would miss some office time for recruiting and road trips, I needed the support and approval of my boss, the dean of students, before we could talk seriously about the job. I made my way as quickly as possible to my boss's office. When I told him of my good fortune, he just started to frown, wave his hands, and shake his head. "It just won't work," he grumbled. "We need you here in the office. If you're gone, I'll have to do extra work and I simply can't do that. We're all too busy as it is, so you'll need to decide—the coaching job (paying $2500 a year) or your current job (with a far more substantial salary, housing on campus, health insurance, and retirement benefits), but you can't do both." The choice was obvious, but nonetheless painful. I went back to the AD, thanked him for his confidence in me, and declined to pursue the offer. My hope was that the next head coach would want me to stay on as his assistant.

Several weeks later, the college called a press conference to introduce the new head coach. I slipped into the back of the room to watch the proceedings. The president stepped to the mic and announced that after an exhausting national search, they had found the perfect candidate for the job. He turned to his left and pointed to the new head basketball coach, my boss, the dean of students. I was absolutely stunned. I couldn't believe it. I felt betrayed and deeply disappointed. I realized that while he was out of the office on recruiting and road trips, I would be the one answering phones and picking up the slack in the office. It was so unfair. I had a full-time job myself! And it suddenly hit me that since I would be doing some the dean's job so he could coach, I would not be able to continue as the assistant coach. I was out of coaching altogether.

I had just been dealt a major setback. I was no longer stunned; now I was disillusioned! So much for God's prefect plan—thank you very much. Who was I to trust? I found myself traveling on the other road, the roundabout way of the wilderness, and I was not at all happy about it.

As I look back now, that next year was not an easy one for anyone in the office. I'm sure I let my disappointment and discontent show like a badge of honor on more than one occasion. It was my forty days and forty nights, a time of trial and an unexpected transition. I attended every home game with a critical eye, but, to be fair, the dean was a very good basketball coach, probably better than I would have been. And near the end of that year, I received a job offer out of the blue, an offer that would put me on an entirely new career path. I would never coach again, but in my new job

I developed a deep passion for Christian higher education and a genuine interest in academic administration. After completing a PhD in that area, I began a rewarding career serving as an academic administrator in several Christian universities. To be honest, it is probably more accurate to say that this career found me more than I found it, but I am so thankful that my gifts and talents found new places of service to take root and grow.

So even though my career as a coach ended in a major disappointment, it forced me to look beyond the basketball court and see something new. A fulfilling career emerged, one that I wouldn't trade for anything, but that doesn't mean that it has always been smooth sailing. It rarely is. And there have been other disappointments from time to time. That is the stuff of life.

Near the end of my career, for example, I was wondering about the best way to finish my last years when, out of the blue, an up-and-coming university president called me and wanted to meet with me. He was hoping that I would consider joining his team and serve as provost. It was a prominent university, and I was honored for the interest and excited about the possibility of ending my academic career at such a prestigious institution. It was perfect!

As the day of our meeting approached, I could hardly stand it. And as I put on the shirt and slacks bought for the occasion, I couldn't stop grinning at myself in the mirror. I was still grinning when I met my friend and future boss at the front door of a very posh restaurant. After some small talk, he told me a bit about what was going on at the university and what he wanted in the next provost, but I could see that his heart was not in it. There was no energy in his words. It turned out to be a very short lunch, and he never asked me a question—not even one. I'm pretty good at reading people and situations, and I knew that this job opportunity was not going to happen. I told my wife later that afternoon that when he looked at me, I could tell that he thought I was a bit too old, beyond my prime, maybe over the hill. I wouldn't get the job. Now, I don't know if that was the case or not, but I do know that he never got in touch with me again. Crickets.

Of course, I was deeply disappointed. It took a full forty days and nights to get the picture of the president's gaze out of my mind when he looked at me in that restaurant. It hurt me. And then to top it off, the person who was appointed as provost called and wondered if I would serve as his mentor! The irony was not lost on me. I wished him the best but graciously declined the invitation.

So, in a way, I started and ended my career with a deep disappointment. I survived them, of course, but they do leave a mark. Disappointments always do—they shape you, but you can learn from them too. They can change you for the better, making you more sensitive to the disappointments others face in their own forty days and nights. I do hope that I am. And when you compare my disappointments to the disappointments that Moses faced, I have very little to complain about. He was the original traveler on the roundabout way of the wilderness, and it was quite a trip!

MOSES: THE ROUNDABOUT WAY OF THE WILDERNESS—TRAVELING THE OTHER ROAD

On the other road, indeed. Moses was born in Egypt and was left in a basket along the backwaters of the Nile where the daughter of Pharaoh found him and adopted him as her own. For all we know, Moses was raised and educated in the Egyptian court, growing up in extreme luxury and privilege, but it seems he never forgot where he came from. One day, while overlooking the Hebrew's hard labor, he saw an Egyptian beating a worker, and after "looking this way and that and seeing no one, he killed the Egyptian and hid him in the sand" (Exod 2:12). However, someone did see him and reported him to the authorities. When Pharaoh got wind of the crime, he wanted him dead, so Moses fled to Midian—not exactly next door. He was forty years old.

When he first arrived in Midian, he intervened in a water dispute between the daughters of Jethro, the local priest, and some angry shepherds. As a result, Moses was invited to move in with the priest's family where he began working as a shepherd himself, and eventually took one of the priest's daughters for his wife. When his first son was born, however, he named him Gershon (meaning *a foreigner there*) and said, "I have become a foreigner in a foreign land" (Exod 2:22). You can hear the estrangement and loneliness in his voice—he didn't belong there, or in Egypt, or anywhere for that matter, and herding sheep for a living wasn't exactly the privileged occupation he foresaw while growing up in Egypt. No home, no heritage, and no vocation—but all that would eventually change.

Forty years later, when Moses saw a burning bush out in the hills and met God there, they had quite a conversation. God wanted to rescue his people from Egyptian forced labor and give them a new homeland. He wanted Moses to take the lead in doing so. Understandably, Moses was not too excited. After all, he fled Egypt with a murder warrant out for him, but God told him that those who wanted to kill him were no longer alive. He was concerned that the Hebrews would not readily recognize him or acknowledge his leadership, but God promised to send along some signs and wonders to use that would gain their trust. He worried that he didn't have the eloquence to speak for the Hebrews, but God promised that his brother, Aaron, would serve as his spokesperson. In fact, Aaron was already headed his way. And Moses worried that Pharaoh would not be open to the idea of a Hebrew liberation and exodus, but God promised that a series of severe plagues would change Pharaoh's mind, if need be.

By then, God was growing impatient with Moses' foot dragging. Moses finally agreed to go and set out with his family in tow for Egypt. Along the way, however, God almost killed Moses, apparently because his son was uncircumcised. Fortunately, at the last minute, his wife, Zipporah, took a flint knife, circumcised their son, and used his foreskin as part of a rather strange ceremony. It saved the day (Exod 4:24–26), but they were not off to the best of starts!

When Moses and Aaron arrived in Egypt, all Moses' worries were realized, but through the series of signs, wonders, and plagues that God had promised to provide for them, they eventually won the day. Pharaoh let the people go and they left, taking the bones of their patriarch, Joseph, with them. Just before he died, Joseph made the Israelites promise: "God will surely come to your aid, and then you must carry my bones up with you from this place" (Exod 13:19b). Clearly, Joseph anticipated the exodus and did not want to be left behind in Egypt. He wasn't. His bones were on the other road too.

Moses must have been euphoric but totally exhausted as they departed, thinking back on all the turmoil but grateful that it was now behind them. Little did he know the frustrations and setbacks just around the bend on the wilderness road.

To begin with, crossing the Sea of Reeds (Red Sea) with Pharaoh's army in hot pursuit was no picnic, but with the help of a pillar of cloud, a pillar of fire, and a guiding angel, they made their way. By now, you would think that Moses had solidified his leadership among the Hebrew people and demonstrated God's presence among them, but this was not the case. The Hebrews proved to be a band of bitter complainers. They complained about the drinking water on more than one occasion, and the lack of food too, and when God provided both, they still weren't satisfied. They didn't follow instructions forbidding the hoarding of food and paid a terrible price for it. And they bickered and fought with each other all the time. In fact, Moses sat to adjudicate their disputes from daylight to dark, but it was never enough. And then out of the blue, the Amalekites attacked—from behind, as was their custom. The Hebrews carried the battle as long as Moses faced the invaders and held up his hands, which he did until sunset by sitting on a stone and having Aaron and Hur assist him, each holding up one of his arms. This was more than Moses bargained for.

Fortunately, help arrived. Moses received word that his father-in-law, Jethro, was coming out to the wilderness to see him, and he was bringing Moses' entire family with him. When Moses recounted all the Lord had done in Egypt and in the wilderness, Jethro was delighted and said: "Praise be to the Lord. . . . Now I know that the Lord is greater than all other Gods. . . . Then Jethro, Moses' father-in-law, brought a burnt offering and other sacrifices to God, and Aaron came with all the elders of Israel to eat a meal with Moses' father-in-law in the presence of God" (Exod 18:10–12). Jethro also gave Moses some sage advice about how to organize in order to avoid trying to settle every complaint himself. It really helped.

What a wonderful conclusion to a long and trying journey on the other road. His family gathered around him. He received wise counsel and a blessing from his father-in-law, a priest, and Aaron and all the elders of Israel acknowledged both his leadership and God's presence in their midst. They affirmed the new covenant with an oath and a ceremony. And Moses was no longer a foreigner in a foreign land, but the established and honored leader of a people who were free and on the way to a new land. As they gathered at the foot of Mount Sinai to meet with God, what could possibly go wrong?

FORTY DAYS AND FORTY NIGHTS: ON TOP OF THE MOUNTAIN

God was not just present, leading the Israelites to a new home, but desirous of a deeper relationship with them as well, different from the covenant with Abraham. That was more of a promise, a summons, a one-way commitment on God's part to Abraham and future generations of his family to give them a homeland. As the Letter to the Hebrews puts it: "By faith Abraham, when called to go to a place he would later receive as his inheritance, obeyed and went, even though he did not know where he was going. By faith he made his home in the promised land like a stranger in a foreign land" (Heb 11:8–9). A stranger in a foreign land—sounds a bit like Moses—but God expected more from the Israelites: "I will walk among you and be your God, and *you will be my people*" (Lev 26:12, italics added). So, there were expectations and obligations for the Israelites too, and as it turns out, a great many of them!

There were instructions regarding who would be involved in leading and participating in various religious ceremonies, what kinds of sacrifices were acceptable, when offerings were to be brought, where different religious activities were to take place, and how to conduct themselves as a people. Perhaps the centerpiece of these communal expectations given to Moses by God was what is now known as the Ten Commandments, a list of community standards and expectations, if you will, intended to guide and shape the Israelites' life together. It was a long and daunting list, and it is easy to understand that the Israelites might have felt that it was a bit too much, more than they had bargained for. We don't really know, but we do know what happened next, and it almost overturned the apple cart.

Moses went up on the mountain and conversed with God for the next forty days and nights—a long time, a formative time, and simply a wonderful time too—for Moses. For the Israelites, not so much. They didn't know if Moses had deserted them or died on the mountain or just decided to live up there. However, they did know that the very first commandment that God gave Moses was: "I am the Lord your God, who brought you out of Egypt, out of the land of slavery. You shall have no other gods before me" (Exod 20:2-3). But at the very time that Moses received the Ten Commandments (the Covenant Law) in writing (on two tablets) and started down the mountain, the Israelites were singing and dancing around a golden calf—a god of their own making. This was a clear repudiation of the very first commandment, and a clear repudiation of Moses' leadership too. It was almost more than Moses could take, a major-league setback. After leading the Israelites out of Egypt, putting up with their grumbling and groaning, and spending the richest and most rewarding forty days and nights of his spiritual life on the mountain top with God, he returns to a bitter disappointment. His people rejected his leadership, violated the very first of God's explicit expectations by embracing another form of worship, and to top it off, his brother, Aaron, was leading the entire pagan celebration!

Moses must have felt this bitter disappointment to the core, and he was angry too! He threw down the tablets and broke them into pieces. So much for the covenant. No one would have blamed him if he had just stomped off in disgust, packed up his tent, and went back to Midian. I think that's what most of us would have done, but he didn't. Of course, there would be consequences for their disobedience, and yet, rather than packing his tent and going home in the face of a major setback, Moses went back up the mountain and pleaded with God on their behalf, and on his behalf too. It took some doing and a lot of negotiating, but in the end, Moses received a new set of stone tablets and God's promise to lead them on to the land of Canaan. That took forty days and nights too. It was grace in action.

Facing the most bitter disappointment of his life, Moses went back up the mountain and met God. When setbacks come, sometimes that's all you can do. Sometimes you can't go forward until you go back.

FORTY DAYS AND FORTY NIGHTS: ON THE CUSP OF SOMETHING BIG

The journey to the border of Canaan was filled with several unanticipated events: fire and dark clouds coming down from above, a sprouting staff, a talking donkey, quail and manna in abundance, water flowing from a rock, and a mutiny led by Moses' own family, to name just a few. Still, they arrived in the vicinity of Canaan, and the people met with Moses and suggested that he should send some spies to explore the land before they all went forward. I think they were setting Moses up for a fall, but he didn't see it coming. As Moses later reflected on the event, "The idea seemed good to me" (Deut 1:23a). What could possibly go wrong? So, Moses gave these instructions: "Go up through the Negev and on into the hill country. See what the land is like and whether the people who live there are strong or weak, few or many. What kind of land do they live in? Is it good or bad? What kind of towns do they live in? Are they unwalled or fortified? How is the soil? Is it fertile or poor? Are there trees in it or not? Do your best to bring back some the fruit of the land" (Num 13:17b–20a).

The twelve spies departed in pairs to explore the land. Can you imagine the excitement that Moses must have felt as he watched the spies move off in pairs and out of sight. They were so close to the end of the journey, on the cusp of something really big, the promised land! He wanted some details so he could fashion a crossing plan and think about what kind of life they could establish on this new land. And he must have been even more excited when he saw their silhouettes on the horizon after forty days and forty nights. Surely he was eager to hear the news, but instead of bringing back a factual report as Moses had instructed them, ten spies came back with their own assessment of the situation, and it was not a good one. They reported that there were large and fortified cities, and the land was inhabited by giants that made them feel like grasshoppers. Hearing this report, the Israelites began to grumble, raising their voices and weeping: "If only we had died in Egypt! Or in this wilderness! Why is the Lord bringing us to this land only to let us fall by the sword? . . . We should choose a leader and go back to Egypt" (Num 14:2–4).

Go back to Egypt—to slavery? Are you kidding me? Moses must have been beside himself. After all they had been through and all the ways that God had led them, protected them, and supplied their needs, *now* they want to go back to captivity? It was an unbelievable setback. And even though Moses, Joshua, and Caleb did quell the talk of a return to Egypt, the Lord told Moses that as a result of the Israelites' disbelief, not one of them over the age of twenty would possess the promised land. They would all wander in the wilderness for another forty years. Forty more years!!

Now Moses was not just feeling the disappointment of a bitter setback. This was much worse—he was to spend the next forty years leading a people who turned their backs on his leadership, and on God's promises too. He had to walk with these folk, live with these folk, care for these folk. No, this wasn't just disappointing; it was full-blown despair. And there was no way this time to go back to the mountain and ask for a do-over, to start over. Facing a public setback that brought unexpected disappointment, rejection, despair, and embarrassment too, Moses had to keep going, showing up each day. He was on the cusp of something big, they all were, but through no fault of his own it didn't happen, and wouldn't happen for another forty years. All the spies saw the same land. Two came back and said, "With God's help, we can do this!" Ten looked at the same reality and said, "We are grasshoppers in their eyes, and we feel like grasshoppers too. We can't do it!" They wanted to stay in the wilderness, and they carried the day.

How he controlled his anger and dealt with his own despair, I do not know. He could have packed up his tent and headed back to Midian, but he didn't. Moses kept showing up day after day after day for the next forty years until once again they were near the river. Canaan was on the other side. When setbacks come, sometimes you can't go back for a do-over. You have to keep moving forward as best you can, one step at a time. Sometimes that's all you can do.

CROSSING THE JORDAN: DISILLUSIONED

If the setback with the golden calf brought discouragement and the Israelites refusal to claim the promised land brought bitter despair, you would hope that Moses had seen the worst of it, but there was still one more setback to face on the other road—disillusionment. At this point, Moses was an old man, and after all that he had been through since his conversation with God at the burning bush, there was only one thing that he wanted to do—lead his people into the promised land. It had been a long road marked by one setback and frustration after another, but here they were on the banks of the river. He was ready to lead them across, but God had other plans. It would be Joshua who would do the honors, he was told. "What? Are you kidding?" Moses must have thought, "Joshua, my assistant, this intern, will become the leader?"

Naturally, Moses pleaded and pleaded and pleaded with God to reconsider. We do not know how long he pleaded with God, but I suspect that it was for forty days and forty nights. Finally, God said, "Do not speak to me anymore about this matter. Go up to the top of Pisgah and look west and north and south and east. Look at the land with your own eyes, since you are not going to cross this Jordan. But commission Joshua, and encourage and strengthen him, for he will lead this people across and will cause them to inherit the land that you will see" (Deut 3:26b–28).

Losing your illusions can be painful, and in this case, I'm sure it was for Moses. He was operating under the illusion that he was the only one who could lead this band of nomads, and after all he had been through, he deserved to be the leader at the crossing of the river. God owed him that much for his loyalty. It was his right to lead the people, but God relieved Moses of that illusion. In the end, God will do what God will do, and we don't have any right to expect or demand a leadership position because we deserve it. As it turns out, we don't. Leadership in God's kingdom is a privilege, but not because we are privileged. It doesn't work that way.

Yet another setback, this time a big one, perhaps the biggest one, certainly the last one. So, what did Moses do? He could have packed up his tent and gone home. Who would have blamed him? But he didn't. The details are thin here, but this is what I think happened. Moses pressed his lips together, nodded his head, wiped away a tear or two, cleared his throat, and softly said, Ok. Then, he called his leadership council together and commissioned Joshua as the new leader with all the dignity and enthusiasm he could muster, and behind the scenes, he encouraged and supported Joshua every way he could. Disillusioned and hurt, but with grace and dignity, Moses honored the God who had been with him every step of the journey, though every setback on the other road, the roundabout way of the wilderness. That's what true leaders do. The first obligation of a leader is to lift the human spirit; the last obligation is to make a graceful exit. Well done, Moses!

CLOSING COMMENTS

There are several important takeaways from the story of Moses that are applicable to our lives. We don't always get to choose the roads we travel, perhaps not very often at all. How many times have we had things all planned out only to find ourselves, like Moses, traveling on the roundabout road of the wilderness, a road with its share of setbacks, difficulties, rejection, and sometimes despair? Haven't we all pleaded with God at one time or another? More often than not, however, the road finds us more than we find the road. I believe that we are called to be faithful and to embrace the journey with all its twists and turns. Our path won't resemble the long entry boulevard leading into an amusement park. I wish it did, but life doesn't work that way. It seems like just when things are going our way, the Amalekites attack—always from behind and often close to home. We each have our own stories to tell.

Setbacks will come to most of us, sometimes more than once. After forty days and nights on the mountain top, the reality of life sets in, but a setback doesn't mean that we are on the wrong road or that God doesn't love us anymore. It does mean that there is some spiritual work to do, whether it is to go back and make things right when you can, just keep going in the face of bitter disappointments, or stop and follow the leading of the Holy Spirit, even if it means bowing out of some responsibility or letting go of some activity or position that you have your heart set on. Remember, God will do what God will do. It's about the kingdom, not about us.

It is easy to lose the long view on the mountain top too. Moses did. He thought the journey would end when they crossed the Jordan River, but in actuality it was only the start of a very long journey, begun with a promise to Abraham and including all of us today—and it will continue well beyond us too. His job was not to end the journey, but to keep it going.

Sometimes we lose perspective too, thinking a job must be done and we're the only one who can do it, only to find out how easily others step up and step in when we step out of the way. It is easy to live under the illusion that we are the most important person in our small group, in our office, in our neighborhood, in the music program, or on the church board. When we carry that illusion, more likely than not we will find ourselves disillusioned—and in this case, it's not a bad thing.

When the people met with Moses at the river and suggested that he send in some spies before they crossed the river themselves, they didn't really have his best interests in mind. They had an ulterior motive. They were afraid to cross over and claim the promise of a promised land, so they suggested a bit of a ruse, knowing full well how the spies (at least most of them) would respond. It is difficult at times to know when you have friends or when others are just being friendly. Not every smile indicates good intentions.

Maybe that is why Jesus told his disciples, "I am sending you out like sheep among wolves. Therefore be as shrewd as snakes and as innocent as doves" (Matt 10:6). Shrewd and innocent—not always easy, but good advice for all of us.

Finally, the story of Moses teaches us that while life is messy (it either is, has been, or will be), God is faithful—always. On whatever road we find ourselves, God is with us along the way, and when we get to wherever we are going, God is already there and at work, bringing hope and healing and grace to all of us. Our forty days and nights of disappointment and transition are part of the journey, but not the end of the road. Thanks be to God!

CHAPTER TWO

Giants—David

Don't let the giant dictate the terms of engagement.
—PATRICK ALLEN

INTRODUCTION

Since conflicts are inevitable for most of us, I trust that the story of David and Goliath will be instructive. And as we will see, Goliath was not the only giant that David had to face in his lifetime. I have come to believe that the Twenty-Third Psalm (either written by David, or for David, or in honor of David) represents the recollecting of an old and successful giant fighter, thinking back on his journey of faith as one who walked "through the darkest valley" on more than one occasion and knew that he was never alone (Ps 23:4a). Read it and see if you agree.

DAVID AND GOLIATH

Samuel's Visit

The day started out like most other days. David and his seven brothers joined their father, Jesse, for some breakfast before gathering their things and heading out to the fields to relieve the night shepherds who were tending the sheep. But this was not like most other days. Not long after they settled into their usual morning routine, someone came running, yelling, filled with excitement, summoning the family back to the house. Jesse had received a message from no one other than Samuel, the most well-known and respected person in the entire land. He had served in the various roles of prophet, priest, general, and political leader all at the same time until he anointed Saul as king. Samuel made it known that it was against his better judgment, but anoint Saul he did, and even now he was certainly just as popular and influential as the king himself. There were stories about how God used Samuel to keep Saul in line, at least some of the time.

The boys were to come back immediately, take a bath, and put on their best clothes. All the boys, that is, except David, the runt of the family. He was to stay there and watch the sheep, pretending to kill lions and bears with his sling. It was his usual way of entertaining himself, and he was good at it. Rumor had it that Samuel was going to anoint a successor to Saul as the future king, and it would be one of the sons of Jesse! It was more than they could even comprehend. They ran all the way back home.

Samuel arrived, and after the usual courtesies and ceremonies the boys lined up in order of age and, one by one, walked past Samuel, holding their breath the entire time, each hoping that he would be the next king, but Samuel didn't bite. Finally, he asked Jesse if he had any other sons. Reluctantly, a bit embarrassed and not wanting to waste Samuel's time, he said that he had one other son, the youngest, but he was just a kid. When Samuel saw David, however, he recognized him as the real deal and anointed him as the future king on the spot! Scripture doesn't report how his brothers responded, but it doesn't take a genius to imagine that they were shocked, stunned really, confused, probably angry, and wondering if Samuel had lost his mind. And they probably weren't the only ones. Jesse, however, couldn't keep from grinning and chuckling the rest of the day and long into the night.

It seems that the next days and weeks were business as usual. Maybe the brothers teased and made fun of the future king, crafting him a homespun crown to wear in the fields, but more likely than not, they didn't say a word about it, at least not to David. They left him alone, slinging smooth stones at imaginary bears and lions and wolves until it was time to go home. Then one day, out of the blue, Jesse received a rather strange message from King Saul's court. They wanted David to leave his shepherding job and come to the court. He was to play his lyre for King Saul whenever he was in one of his terrible moods, tormented by an evil spirit, something that was happening on a regular basis. How the court knew that David played the lyre or that he was out in the fields with a flock of sheep was never fully explained, but it is likely that the purpose of Samuel's visit to the house of Jesse got back to Saul and his people. After all, it was a tight-knit, connected community, people knew each other, and any bit of information about the anointing of a new king would certainly have been great grist for the rumor mill, and of even greater interest to the reigning king. My guess is that Saul knew exactly what he was doing by inviting David to join his court, keeping his friends close and his potential rivals even closer. Trouble may have been brewing on the horizon, but for now, David won favor in the court and was appointed as one of Saul's armor-bearers, an honored position reserved for those who were brave and cunning. What happened next would require both virtues.

Facing Goliath

Jesse and his sons received word that the Philistines were at it again. "They gathered their forces for war and assembled at Sokoh in Judah" (17:1), 1 Samuel tells us, and Saul and the Israelites gathered their forces too. David's three oldest brothers heeded Saul's call to arms and headed out on a dead sprint, ready to join forces with those men preparing to defend their land. The battle lines were drawn; the Philistines on one hill and the Israelites on another—the Valley of Elah in between. Although both sides yelled, postured, and marched around each day, no one prevailed at enticing the other to attack, thus exposing themselves to a fierce counterattack on their flanks. They were at an impasse, but that would soon change.

A champion named Goliath came out of the Philistine camp and yelled across the valley, "'Why do you come out and line up for battle? Am I not a Philistine, and are you not the servants of Saul? Choose a man and have him come down to me. If he is able to fight and kill me, we will become your subjects; but if I overcome him and kill him, you will become our subjects and serve us.' Then the giant said, 'This day I defy the armies of Israel! Give me a man and let us fight each other.' On hearing the Philistine's words, Saul and all the Israelites were dismayed and terrified" (1 Sam 17:8–11).

Dismayed and terrified, indeed. Who wouldn't be! You see, Goliath was no ordinary fighter. He was gigantic—nine feet nine inches tall, standing in his bare feet, and he wore a massive suit of armor. His shield-bearer could hardly carry his spare equipment and weapons for him. They were huge, and heavy too. The thought of fighting him was simply terrifying. And if that wasn't enough, Goliath came out *every morning and evening* for forty days to taunt the Israelites—*forty days and nights*! I'm sure the taunting took a severe toll on morale too. What were they to do?

And to add insult to injury, the Philistines had changed the terms of engagement in the middle of the conflict. Instead of taking turns attacking each other's battle lines, hoping for a sudden, dramatic breakthrough and victory, the Philistines proposed a one-on-one, winner-take-all contest, and they just happened to have on their side the biggest, meanest-looking, best-equipped warrior for that kind of fight. It wasn't fair. They suddenly changed the rules, and the decks were stacked against the Israelites. What were they to do, indeed!

During all of this, David was working behind the front lines, shuttling back and forth between serving as one of Saul's armor-bearers (Saul stayed behind the front lines too) and going home to help his other brothers tend the flocks. You can just imagine how anxious Jesse was to receive any news about the battle, especially since his three eldest sons were in the thick of it. One morning, as David was preparing to return to Saul's service, Jesse told him to take some roasted grain and loaves of bread for his brothers on the front lines, and ten cheeses for the commander of their unit. It doesn't hurt to stay in the good graces with the one who chooses whom among his troops will lead the charge against the enemy. Just a little insurance, so to speak.

When David arrived, he left the food with the keeper of supplies and headed out to find his brothers on the front line. Just as he arrived, Goliath made his daily morning appearance. As usual, the Israelite army edged back in terror. David didn't understand. If they had God on their side, why were they afraid? Besides, the king promised that anyone who dispatched Goliath would be given great wealth, one of Saul's daughters, and a tax exemption for his family. Wow! If no one else would take up the challenge, maybe he would, he told those standing near him.

Understandably, his older brothers were furious with David. Was he mocking his older brothers, or was he delusional, or had Samuel's anointing gone to his head? They told him that the best thing he could do was to go back to his father and tend what sheep were left in the flock, but just then David was summoned to Saul's tent. Someone overheard their argument and reported it to Saul. David said that with God's help, he would fight and win.

With no one else willing to face the giant, what did Saul have to lose by sending out this boy to fight Goliath? After all, he might pull off a miracle and win. And if David lost his life, so be it. He probably would, and that would be the end of that ugly "anointing" rumor that had been making its way around the royal party. At the very least, they wouldn't be accused of refusing to face the giant any longer. If truth be told, Saul was out of options. He told David: "Go, and the Lord be with you" (1 Sam 17:37b). Apparently, that's the only company that he would have.

In order to present some acceptable optics, David was pressed into wearing Saul's armor, but it simply didn't fit. It was made for a strong, tall warrior, and for a certain type of fighting. He couldn't even move, let alone run around and challenge the giant in hand-to-hand combat. He told them so. In fact, little did they know that David had in mind a totally different approach to fighting the giant, refusing to let the giant dictate the terms of engagement. So, he asked for his staff and his sling. Then he took five smooth stones from a nearby stream and put them in his shepherd's pouch. These were the tools of his craft, and he knew how to use them—he'd practiced all his life.

What happened next was simply amazing. Goliath's shield-bearer carried his gigantic shield in front of him as they approached David. This was not the usual position for an armor-bearer, perhaps indicating that Goliath was shortsighted. Maybe he was there to point out the direction of the advancing fighter. We don't really know, but we do know that Goliath did not see what was coming next—a smooth stone to the middle of the forehead. He fell face down on the ground with a thud, out cold, and before he could recover, David killed the giant with his own sword and cut off his head. Encouraged by the sight of David holding up Goliath's head, the Israelites rushed the Philistines and chased them all the way to the entrance of Gath and to the gates of Ekron. The battle was on—and over. Then they returned and plundered the Philistine camp. Goliath's head was displayed as a warning and reminder on a hill just outside Jerusalem, then a Philistine city. It was a great victory!

Lessons Learned

We all face giants of one kind or another from time to time. It might be an illness, an addiction, an injury to body, mind, or spirit, an abuse, a shattered relationship, a financial disaster, a public failure, a deep loss, or a mean-spirited, small-minded, narcissistic boss, to name just a few. Such giants are rarely invited, and they show up at the most inopportune times, often just when we think we have it all together and our future is bright and beautiful, having earned God's richest blessings. Unfortunately, life doesn't work like that. I wish it did, but it doesn't.

The giants in our lives don't just show up one day and then quietly slip away the next. No, they tend to linger, taunting us, challenging us, fighting us for forty days and forty nights. They have staying power, and they are fueled by uncertainty and fear. We can't ignore them or wish them away. They must be faced, one of the hardest things we will ever do, and we have to be in it for the long haul.

We can't fight the giant in Saul's armor. In other words, you will receive a boatload of advice from well-intentioned friends, family, and neighbors about what you should do or how you should feel or what not to do. What worked for someone's aunt you know from serving together in the food pantry won't necessarily work for you. Every situation is different. Be careful who you listen to and be prepared to fight your own battles. There are no universal answers or strategies.

Like David, you must use your own gifts and graces. When the giant makes an appearance, don't be surprised if you are already prepared to fight the battle. You have transferable skills and prior preparation, and you have more reserves than you know. Look for them. Summon them. Lean on them. And remember, you don't have to fight the battle alone. God is always present and faithful. A close friend is a blessing too.

Don't let the giant dictate the terms of engagement. We often are fooled into thinking that we have to fight the giant on the giant's terms. Not so! Not only do we have unrecognized reserves and untapped resources, but we also have an unquenchable source of faith, hope, and love—powerful weapons in any battle. You get to choose how and when to deploy them, and don't let the giant convince you that they don't matter or don't work. They do, and they do!

Sometimes we must battle more than one giant, or after fighting one giant, another rises up to take its place, sometimes two. It is a difficult reality, but not impossible to overcome. For example, after Goliath, David faced three other giants in succession. We will look at these battles to see what we can learn when these giants make their sudden appearance and taunt us for forty days and nights—maybe longer. Truly, these are trying times, but they can also be times of personal transition and spiritual growth. I believe that Psalm 23 stands as a testimony to the faithfulness of God who prepared a table for David in the midst of his enemies. It is the testimony of a king, a giant fighter, and it can be our testimony too. Thanks be to God!

DAVID AND SAUL

Unanticipated Troubles

When David dispatched Goliath in full view of his older brothers and all of Saul's army, he must have thought that his troubles were over. After all, he was now a hero, saving Saul's bacon, but when the women along the victory-parade route starting dancing and singing, "Saul has slain his thousands, and David his tens of thousands" (1 Sam 18:7), trouble was brewing. Saul didn't like it a bit—"the refrain displeased him greatly" we are told (18:8), and he was both angry with David and afraid of him at the same time. That was not a prescription for a good relationship with an insecure king. Saul vowed to keep a close eye on him. We aren't told in Scripture what that vow meant, but it doesn't take a genius to understand that David was in serious trouble.

It's strange how doing something really brave and good can get you in hot water, especially so if the boss is shepherding and cultivating a fearful and dysfunctional organization with his own narcissism. Acts of courage and deeds of grace often get turned on their heads, and ordinarily healthy relationships and good working conditions quickly go south. They did for David.

On the Run

Fortunately, David and Jonathan, one of Saul's sons, crafted a deep and enduring friendship. During the rest of Saul's reign of delusion and confusion, this friendship served David well, providing personal encouragement, wise counsel, and inside information about what the king was up to and what mood he was in at the time. Saul's moods swung quickly from wanting to embrace David, calling him one of his sons, to wanting to kill him, which he tried to do on a regular basis. When he wasn't trying to kill David with his own spear at the supper table, Saul would send him out to fight the Philistines, hoping that he would be a causality of war. Instead, David came back time after time victorious, making him even more popular with the people and the troops, and Saul more and more inclined to get rid of him.

Saul even offered his daughter, Michal, in marriage if David brought in one hundred Philistine foreskins as the price for his bride. Of course, Saul was hoping that in doing battle with so many Philistines at one time, David would be killed. Instead, he returned with two hundred foreskins and married Michal. It was truly a love affair, and Michal saved David's life on more than one occasion. Even on his darkest days, he could count on Michal and Jonathan. Sometimes during our own forty days and nights that is all we have to hold on to—just a friend or two.

David was constantly on the run to avoid Saul's henchmen, and when he wasn't, he was fighting the Philistines, the Amalekites, and any other enemies who dared to attack Israel. Through all of this, David remained strangely loyal to Saul. He had the opportunity to kill Saul while on the run on more than one occasion, but he didn't. He couldn't. After all, at one time, he was a sworn armor-bearer for him, and he was going to keep his oath, no matter what—a promise was a promise, as he saw it. In the end, Saul, his three sons, his armor-bearer, and all his men died in battle on the same day, and David honestly and bitterly lamented their passing.

Consolidation

After Saul's death, his son Ish-Bosheth became king over Israel, but the tribe of Judah remained loyal to David. Tensions were high, of course, and as Scripture tells us: "The war between the house of Saul and the house of David lasted a long time. David grew stronger and stronger, while the house of Saul grew weaker and weaker" (2 Sam 3:1). After Ish-Bosheth's murder several years later, David methodically consolidated his kingdom, defeated the Philistines, conquered Jerusalem, and set up residence there, calling it (not so humbly) the house of David. He, along with thirty thousand men, brought the ark of God to Jerusalem and put on one of the biggest demonstrations of pure joy ever recorded. It was a very good day! And he even sought out Jonathan's son Mephibosheth and brought him to the palace, not to eliminate the last vestiges of the house of Saul, but to give him a permanent place of honor at the king's table in recognition of his father's friendship and loyalty. It was a move that no one saw coming, a gesture that spoke volumes about the character and integrity of the young king.

But something was missing. As 2 Sam 7 tells it: "After the king was settled in his palace and the Lord had given him rest from all his enemies around him, he said to Nathan the prophet, 'Here I am, living in a house of cedar, while the ark of God remains in a tent. . . .' But that night the word of the Lord came to Nathan, saying: 'Go and tell my servant David, "This is what the Lord says: Are you the one to build me a house to dwell in? . . . I took you from the pasture, from tending the flock, and appointed you ruler over my people Israel. I have been with you wherever you have gone. . . . I will make your name great. . . . I will also give you rest from all your enemies. . . . When your days are over and you rest with your ancestors, I will raise up your offspring to succeed you. . . . He is the one to build a house for my name"'" (2 Sam 7:1–13).

God kept his promise and blessed David as the greatest king of Israel—so much so that Jesus, over a thousand years later, referred to himself as the Son of David—but David was not to build the temple. He was a warrior king and had to fight most of his life, sometimes with rivals, sometimes with family, and sometimes with his own ego, very powerful giants indeed. Solomon, who reigned in peace, would do the honors.

Reflections

Before we move on to face giant number three, what can we learn from David's struggle with a self-absorbed boss who led and promoted a terribly dysfunctional organization, a hurtful one, a spirit-damaging one, something that many of us will have to endure or witness at one time or another in our work life or church (sadly, sometimes both)?

Of course, all the insights we drew from the confrontation with Goliath apply here when we find ourselves in an uninvited conflict with someone in power, a giant of sorts, who would like to see us diminished or gone, but let me offer three additional considerations. When you find yourself in conflict with the giant, one who holds the power in one way or another, you will experience and have to manage a great deal of stress, a great deal.

To do so, life-giving relationships are vital. When fighting this particular giant, you need friends (like Jonathan), partners (like Michal), and trusted allies (like David's troops), people you can talk to, cry with, and share your reality. Sometimes you just need a listening ear, sometimes you need an encouraging pep talk, sometimes you need some inside information, and other times you need a reality check. At all times, it is dangerous for mind and spirit when you are isolated and alone. If you are lucky, some friends and allies will seek you out. If so, great! If not, lift up your head, swallow your pride, and seek out some help. Prayerfully find those who will walk with you. Just be careful, not everyone who seeks you out is a friend. Sadly, sometimes they are an informant. In all new relationships, go slowly.

Also, during times of ongoing stress, routine and self-care practices are essential for your well-being. Maintain a regular time each day for physical exercise, eating, sleep, devotions, and periods of silence. Think about bookending your day—beginning each day with the *intention* of seeing God at work, even in the worst places and at the worst times, and ending each day with a sense of *gratitude*. And during the day, take time to get away, maybe at lunch with someone you love or a short drive or walk before returning to work—maybe both. Do it as regularly as you can.

Above all, don't let yourself be drawn into the dysfunction. Keep a healthy orbit above the giant hair ball. Don't succumb to believing that it doesn't matter how you conduct yourself, that you can treat others as you have been treated, that you only have to take care of yourself, or that integrity and honor don't matter. They do;

they always do. When facing a particularly nasty giant, maintaining your integrity and keeping your word may be all that you will be able to salvage from the experience. That's ok; that's enough.

DAVID AND NATHAN

If it is true that we are shaped by the stories we tell, and I think it is, what does it say about us when we remember and tell stories about King David? For most children, it is the story of David and Goliath, how David, with bravery and cunning, used his own gifts and graces to face the giant, subdue him, and cut off his head. It is truly a remarkable story of a simple shepherd who rose to the heights of power and became a great king, a true hero, an example for all of us.

For many adults, perhaps most, however, it is not the story of David and Goliath that is remembered. Rather, it is the story of David and Bathsheba—not the story of the simple shepherd who rose to the heights of power, but rather a powerful leader's fall from grace when he used his power and misused his privilege to get what he wanted, even though he knew that it clearly crossed the line out of moral bounds. Why? For some of us, there is a great curiosity to learn all the sordid details of another's fall, particularly when their life is public, proud, and influential. We somehow feel that they are a bit too big for their britches and their public persona a bit too good to be true, and they are finally receiving what they deserve. In some odd way, it makes us feel better about ourselves.

For others, the story comes too close to home. When we say, "There but for the grace of God go I," we mean it. We all have a dark side, I believe, but for most of us it doesn't come to light in any public way—whether by the grace of God, the mercy of God, unforeseen circumstances, or just plain blind luck, I don't know, but I do know that many of us purse our lips and say a prayer expressing thanks that we aren't the one enduring forty days and nights of public shame and disgrace.

Still others watch from a distance as organizations close ranks around their "mistreated" leader, denying and lashing out at anyone who dares challenge their narrative of reality, but then slowly having the awkward truth come to light. Often, after a period of denials and excuses, the leader takes a long vacation to spend more time with their family. They rarely return.

David's story is different in one major way. The giant who challenged David this time was Nathan the prophet, and he brought with him the most powerful weapon known to us all—the truth. After being confronted, David, the most notable person in his own world, could have gone into damage control and denial, hiding behind a bevy of lawyers and advisors, and having Nathan discredited, exiled, or even killed. Of course, he could have, but he didn't this time. Perhaps he learned from his last attempt at a cover-up involving Bathsheba's husband that only made things more complicated and much worse, a total moral disaster. In any case, when Nathan spoke truth to power at great personal risk, David simply bowed his head and quietly said, "I have sinned against the Lord" (2 Sam 12:13a). He acknowledged that Nathan was right and offered no excuses—none. The giant won the day. There are some giants that you just don't fight.

In the end, although his kingdom was spared, there were consequences for his actions. Some may think that his punishment didn't fit the crime, that he got off too easy, and maybe he did, but for the rest of his life, I don't think a day went by when David didn't think about that sordid affair and subsequent murder with regret. (If you are unfamiliar with the story of David and Bathsheba, see 2 Sam 11–12.)

Psalm 51, subtitled *A Psalm of David*, speaking about David's affair with Bathsheba, puts it this way: "Have mercy on me, O God, according to your unfailing love; according to your great compassion blot out my transgressions. Wash away all my iniquity and cleanse me from my sin. . . . You do not delight in sacrifice, or I would bring it; you do not take pleasure in burnt offerings. My sacrifice, O God, is a broken spirit; a broken and contrite heart you, God, will not despise" (51:1–2, 16–17). A broken spirit and a contrite heart. That's all David had to offer. It was enough.

Lessons Learned

I think it is important to acknowledge that unchecked power gets good people into trouble almost every time. They begin to think that they can do whatever they want with impunity, that they play by a different set of rules, that they deserve to be treated with special benefits and favors, and that since the organization belongs to them, they can use its resources in any way they see fit. In fact, they see no distinction between their own selves and the organization! Unrestrained power is one of the most corruptive and corrosive forces we know. Good organizations acknowledge this and build in checks and balances accordingly. We need to do the same in our personal and family lives too. The motto is: Power with, not power over.

And when we are confronted with the truth of our transgressions, we must acknowledge them and humbly repent, no matter how awkward and embarrassing or painful or public they are. Our first inclination, of course, is to deny, cover up, lash out, and fight, but in the end, it only adds insult to injury. It corrupts our souls. And even though coming with a broken spirit and offering a contrite heart will not make everything magically disappear, and it shouldn't, it is the pathway leading to forgiveness and renewal. It is usually a hard, long journey, best managed one step at a time.

DAVID AND FAMILY

As we have witnessed, David faced many giants throughout his life—Goliath, Saul, and Nathan, to name just three—but there was one last giant to face, perhaps the most persistent and certainly the most painful one of all—his own family. Families have memory, and conflicts don't simply happen and then disappear. They have staying power, partly because, as time passes, hurtful conflicts are remembered differently or largely ignored or vigorously denied. And sooner or later there is an event or holiday that pulls the family together, and all the injuries and anger and hurt come dressed for the occasion, some just spoiling for a fight. All it takes is for one innocent comment or gesture (or the absence of an expected one) to be misconstrued, and emotions explode. Although time is said to be a great healer, I'm not sure it applies to family conflicts. They are giants that keep coming back to the fight for more. They linger. They love the forty days and nights. As David's own family drama unfolds in 2 Samuel, twice we find these words to introduce a portion of his story: "In the fullness of time" (2 Sam 13:1; 15:1). It's not there by accident.

His family was a mess, and at least a good share of the blame must be laid at his own feet. Sadly, when children are raised in absolute privilege, given unquestioned power, and shaped by dreadful role models, at some point or another they turn inward and fight among themselves. In David's own family there were instances of conceit, selfishness, lust, incest, rape, even murder.

To compound the family dysfunction even more, at various times two of David's sons tried to overthrow the government and seize power from him. On one occasion, David had to leave Jerusalem and flee for his life! If the revolt had been successful, that would have been the end of David and those close to him. After all, you don't let an overthrown king and company just move into the retirement center next door. Yet, when his son Absalom was killed while doing battle with David's own protectors, David grieved publicly and honestly. Why? Because he loved his son, that's why. And this is what makes fighting the giant of a dysfunctional family or an embittered relationship so challenging, because mixed with the pain, hurt, and betrayal are good memories, kinship, and love. For David, the longer he lived, the more complex and confusing family relationships became for everyone involved.

Back to Absalom. On the day he was killed by the king's forces, David grieved publicly. It was an expression of a father's love, of course, but it sent the wrong message to his troops. It was, to say the least, a slap in the face to those loyal and willing to fight for him, and it was more than his general, Joab, could take. He marched into the palace and chastised the king, saying: "You made it clear today that the commanders and their men mean nothing to you. . . . Now go out and encourage your men. I swear by the Lord that if you don't go out, not a man will be left with you by nightfall.

This will be worse for you than all the calamities that have come on you from your youth till now" (2 Sam 19:1–7).

And what did David do? Thankfully, he listened. "So the king got up and took his seat in the gateway. When the men were told, 'the king is sitting in the gateway,' they all came before him" (19:8). Disaster diverted.

Fighting the Giant Called Family—A Few Thoughts

David was by no means a perfect man, but when he was confronted for his misdeeds and mistakes, even sins, by trusted truth tellers, he listened and responded humbly. This is perhaps the greatest strength of this great king. We all need to have those around us who will speak the truth to us, and we need to have the humility to hear what they are telling us and the courage and character to respond accordingly. Fighting a long-standing family giant can distort our vision of reality. We need others to help us find our way.

Unlike losing a friend or a job, some family conflicts have no ending date. There is no final closure. In a way, it can be a death without a funeral. At the very least, this eventuality needs to be recognized and given its own space. Pain and hurt can linger unacknowledged for years, only to erupt at the most unlikely and unexpected times.

The key is to minimize the potential for conflict and to look for small ways to make some progress, microsteps toward restoration, knowing full well that it may never be totally resolved. In such cases, we have to give ourselves permission to live out our lives on our owns terms and leave the heavy lifting to the Holy Spirit.

When we do, sometimes out of nowhere the giant will surrender or call a truce. Accept the white flag and move on together—cautiously. This is not the same thing as trying to go back to how it was. In many ways, there is no "how it was" to return to—and that's ok.

FORTY DAYS AND FORTY NIGHTS

CLOSING COMMENTS

The giants that confront us rarely give advance warning, and they don't just slink quickly and quietly away—they stay for forty days and forty nights, times of hardship *and* spiritual growth. The key, I believe, is to keep the giants and others from dictating the terms of engagement. We must make the ground rules and be ever mindful that there are no paint-by-number kits for our battles with the giants we face. Above all else, we have the promise that God is with us, always, preparing a table for us in the presence of our giants. We never fight alone. Thanks be to God!

Let me leave you with this prayer from *Forward Day by Day*, a daily devotional published by Forward Movement. It is my favorite go-to prayer when fighting a giant. In fact, I pray this prayer at the start of every day. You never know what giant might greet you after lunch.

> For Today
> O God:
> Give me strength to live another day;
> Let me not turn coward before its difficulties
> or prove recreant to its duties;
> Let me not lose faith in other people;
> Keep me sweet and sound of heart,
> in spite of ingratitude, treachery, or meanness;
> Preserve me from minding little stings or giving them;
> Help me to keep my heart clean, and to live
> so honestly and fearlessly that no outward failure can
> dishearten me or take away the joy of conscious integrity;
> Open wide the eyes of my soul that I may see good
> in all things;
> Grant me this day some new vision of thy truth;
> Inspire me with the spirit of joy and gladness;
> and make me the cup of strength to suffering souls;
> in the name of the strong Deliverer, our only Lord
> and Savior, Jesus Christ. Amen.[1]

---

1. "For Today." *Forward Day by Day* 90 (2024) inside back cover. Used by permission.

CHAPTER THREE

Floods—Noah

As long as the earth endures, seedtime and harvest, cold and heat, summer and winter, day and night, shall not cease.

—GEN 8:22

INTRODUCTION

AFTER FORTY DAYS AND forty nights of rain, the floods came and changed everything for Noah—everything. All of us will be hit by a flood at one time or another, and when it starts raining, it is too late to build an ark. Without an ark, we are left to cobble together a life raft as best we can to ride out the storm and make a safe landing somewhere—anywhere. In this chapter, we'll look at both the adult and the Vacation Bible School (VBS) version of the great flood story and why asking difficult questions is so important for our faith development. I'll share a deeply personal time when a major flood (cancer) hit too close to home and offer some insights about what to do when the floods hit us full in the face, whether we have built an ark before the floods come or must patch together a life raft as best we can. Before we close, we'll consider what it means to start all over again in the flood's aftermath. It's not always a pretty picture.

Forty Days and Forty Nights

THE BIBLICAL ACCOUNT OF NOAH: GENESIS 6–9

The Vacation Bible School Version

Children love the story of Noah and the ark almost as much as we love to teach it to them. We have picture books, posters, puzzles, wall plaques, room decor, pillows, mobiles, dinner plates, dolls, play sets, kites, coloring books, videos and movies, to mention only some of the ways the story of Noah and the ark are taught. Most of all, children love the animals—pictures and coloring books show them coming from all over the world, lining up two by two, marching up the path, and happily loading into the ark. There are a lot from Africa: giraffes, elephants, lions, hippos, rhinos, and antelopes. There is usually a convenient window for the giraffes and elephants to use to look out and enjoy the scenery too, and they do. Sometimes an opening in the roof does the trick. Interestingly, there are much fewer barn animals and very few pigs and snakes, even though God told Noah to bring pairs of both clean and unclean animals into the ark (Gen 7:2).

Many pictures show no people at all, and if they do, it is always Noah, and occasionally his family. When we see them, they are *very* happy—they have big smiles and Noah is often pictured with his arms waving wildly in the air. It is difficult to know if the wave is an expression of joy for all that is happening or an act of worship. It could possibly be both.

We do know from almost every storybook that God chose Noah because he loved God, obeyed his commands, and didn't fight, steal, or live unkindly like his neighbors, and, in fact, like all other humans on earth. Their misbehavior made God very sad. As a result, God decided to cause a flood over all the earth, wipe out everyone and everything, and start over again with Noah, his family, and the animals that made it into the ark. As the floodwaters mounted, the ark proved to be seaworthy, and after months and months and months, all disembarked from the ark under sunny skies and a beautiful rainbow, signifying that God would never again destroy the entire world by a flood. In a nutshell, that's what we teach in VBS, a Disneyland version of sorts.

The Adult Version

Paul Harvey, an American radio broadcaster and commentator for ABC News Radio, was a gifted storyteller. His most popular show was *The Rest of the Story*. He would share a story, and at the end, provide some interesting, largely unknown facts so we would all know "the rest of the story." When it comes to Noah and the ark, there is a "rest of the story" to tell too, and I wish it was told and thought about more than it is. I'm afraid that when the floods of life come our way, and they will, the Disneyland version of the great flood will not have enough depth to speak to us when we are trying to comprehend what just happened to us and we are faced with starting over. We need to develop a faith that is mature and strong enough and, dare I say, wise enough to journey with us and carry us during the trials, hardships, and disasters of one kind or another that come our way. Some can be anticipated, some cannot, but all need to be negotiated. They cannot just be ignored or wished away.

So, what does the adult version contain that is largely ignored in VBS? Here's a short list from Genesis, accompanied by a brief question or commentary for each of us to consider:

1. "There were giants in the earth in those days; and also after that." (Gen 6:4a). Since Gen 6 introduces the story of Noah, doesn't "also after that" refer to the great flood, and if so, how did the giants survive? We are told that only those in the ark did so. If "also after that" does not refer to the flood, what is it referring to? And how do we read this text about giants who show up from time to time in the Old Testament? Is anyone searching for their remains or evidence of their villages?

2. In the VBS version of the story, God is *sad* that the human race turned out so terrible. Genesis 6:6–7 tells us, "The LORD regretted that he had made human beings on the earth, and his heart was deeply troubled. So the LORD said, 'I will wipe from the face of the earth the human race I have created—and with them the animals, the birds and the creatures that move

along the ground—for I regret that I have made them.'" Being so deeply troubled that you want to wipe out the human race along with all the animals from the face of the earth seems to me to be a good deal more than just feeling sad. What does this story tell us about the writer's understanding of God's character? After all, didn't God create all these humans in God's own image in the first place? If so, doesn't it seem over the top to just do away with the entire population? How do we understand God's reaction to the human condition?

3. When the ark was full of animals and supplies, Gen 7:16 tells us, the Lord closed the door, shutting them in. Why? Considering the likelihood that others would beg and try to get in to save themselves, what does this mean? Was this to absolve Noah from the genocide that was about to take place outside the ark, or was it to keep Noah from throwing open the door and letting others in, or . . .? Why did the Lord shut them in?

4. Genesis 7:23 reports that "every living thing on the face of the earth was wiped out." Every living thing! Why? Why all the animals and insects? What did they do? Were their lives also somehow tainted by original sin? And later, when God made a covenant with Noah to never again cause a worldwide flood, the covenant was extended to the animals too. Why? What role in the new creation did animals play? And what about now?

5. Something must be said about Noah's voyage in the ark. It couldn't have been easy. When preaching about Noah, a popular preacher's witticism is, "If it weren't for the storm outside, Noah couldn't have endured the stench inside." Of course, there is a good deal of truth in this comment. After all, they were shut up in the ark and couldn't go out for a walk. And floating around in the ark brought its own challenges too. There was no way to steer the ark or navigate on the seas, even if there was a safe harbor somewhere. They were at the mercy of the currents and the winds. And it was a long, long journey. Forty days and nights of rain, then flooding and

destruction, then floating helplessly on the seas for months, and finally starting over in a new place with precious few resources and very little communal or extended family support. It had to be a long, hard rebuild.

6. Honestly, the story of Noah doesn't end very well. In fact, we find him sleeping in his tent, drunk and naked, after which he curses one of his sons for misbehavior. There were good reasons for Noah to be disillusioned and depressed too. Given that fact that almost everything he knew had been wiped out, I get it. That's what floods do. They take away so much, too much, too quickly. He had to start over, but without his friends, his neighbors, his home, or his life as he knew it. Starting over takes courage, resolve, and faith and it doesn't always have a fairy-tale ending.

7. If we look beyond the flood story for just a moment, we see the story of the tower of Babel in the very next chapter (Gen 11). One might wonder if the desire for a reset worked out exactly as God intended. How do we explain humanity's persistent self absorption and arrogance?

8. The rainbow was a beautiful reminder that God would not destroy the world via flood ever again. That must have been helpful to Noah, but there were other ways that God could wipe humankind off the face of the earth—fire, drought, disease, or war, to name just a few. However, there was another promise that God gave to Noah, largely overshadowed by the popularity and prominence of the rainbow but a powerful promise nonetheless, perhaps even more so: "As long as the earth endures, seedtime and harvest, cold and heat, summer and winter, day and night will never cease" (Gen 8:22). What a wonderful promise! When we are in the midst of a flood or struggling in its aftermath, whether it is a loss of our health, our job, our home, our identity, our spouse or loved one, our community, our spirit, our dignity, even our faith, God promises that life will go on—seedtime and harvest, winter and summer, night and day. It is the knowledge that

the flood is not the end, and God is with us. The sun will rise tomorrow, and Providence will rise before the sun. In spite of everything, God refuses to give up on us.

Now you know the rest of the story! Unfortunately, when we tell Noah's story and wrap it up in a beautiful bow, it loses much of its power and significance. The story is complex, difficult, confusing, and at times troubling, but also full of promise, depth, and insight far beyond a rainbow begging to be colored and displayed on the refrigerator.

Please hear me. I am not suggesting in any way that we should push children to engage Scripture like an adult, although I do think a twelve-year-old is far more capable of understanding the nuances of Scripture than we often think. No, my concern is for adults who still cling to the VBS version of the stories in Scripture. I'm not arguing for children to act like mature Christians with a discerning faith, but I am arguing that it is unhelpful, even dangerous, for adults to read Scripture and approach it like a child attending VBS. Grappling with deep and honest questions about Scripture is never a threat to our faith. Rather, it is a practice that will help shape and anchor a mature faith in our God that is buoyant enough to float like an ark when the floods of life come our way, and deep enough to sustain us after the waters reside and we must begin to begin again.

WHEN THE FLOODS COME CLOSE TO HOME

A Bad Rest of This Year

It came out of the blue. Floods always do. My wife, Lori, went in for her regularly scheduled mammogram and ultrasound on Aug. 4, 2022. The doctor came into the room and said, "We see something very suspicious." Lori responded, "I am a person of faith. We'll get through this." Honestly, she demonstrated more strength and courage than I knew she had, certainly more than I had—and I always thought I was the strong one.

A week later, the biopsy confirmed the doctor's suspicions. When asked for his most candid assessment, he said, "Well, it's probably going to be a bad rest of this year, but the years beyond will be good." He was right on both accounts. For the next two months, with each weekly visit to the cancer center, the news kept getting worse and worse and the necessary treatment more radical. It was like a punch in the gut each time. We left reeling in disbelief, unable to quite comprehend it all, and, like clockwork, a week or so later we would receive another bill for services. It was a devastating one-two punch.

Fortunately, there was an overwhelming outpouring of love, support, and prayers from friends and family. Along the way, a neighbor urged us to consider a meal train during recovery from surgery. We were uneasy about requesting help, even though we had participated in meal trains dozens and dozens of times. It's interesting how easy it is to reach out to others in their time of need, but so difficult to ask for help in our own. We did take our neighbor's advice, and we are so thankful we did. It made the recovery process much easier. And each time a neighbor or friend came to our door with a hot meal, we were humbled and deeply blessed. During a crisis, small acts of kindness are never forgotten.

The surgery and recovery went smoothly, but the decision about postoperative care loomed. Would there also be radiation or chemo or another surgery? The prospects of chemo were absolutely frightening for us. Even though we were committed to doing everything necessary to ensure a healthy future, we just didn't want to walk that road if it could be safely avoided. When we received news that a follow-up surgery was recommended *but no chemo*, we hugged, sang, and danced like children. It was a good day for us.

About a year later, the second surgery was performed successfully, and Lori has made an amazing recovery. As the doctor predicted, the first year was not all that good, but we look forward to many good years to come, and we are so thankful for our friends, family, and the wonderful medical team located in our own hometown.

We do recognize that not all cancer stories have such a happy ending. Some floods are more devastating than others, and many cancer journeys do not end with a trip to Disneyland. We tell our story in full recognition of this fact and pray and grieve for all those who are caught in a flood at this moment or dealing with its aftermath.

Cancer Comments

Along the way, we were told many things and heard many words of advice. Here are a few:

The Diagnosis and Treatment Progression:

- It's just a small spot—probably nothing.
- We'll need to do some more tests.
- Probably just a lumpectomy. Oh, and radiation.
- We have complete cancer care here in town.
- Looks like you may need a single mastectomy.
- Hmm. We see another spot. You may want to consider a double mastectomy.
- We'll need to do some genetic testing.
- In the next twenty-four hours, you need to decide on reconstruction—or not.
- The genetic tests are in. We recommend a second surgery.
- Another test will show if chemo is recommended.
- No chemo needed.
- Another surgery will be required later this year.
- You are released from your doctor's care.
- Still a little worry sneaks in every once in a while.

Words Offered by Friends and Strangers:

- I will be praying for you. (Comforting to know that someone cares and prays for us.)
- Thoughts and prayers to you—as they walk away. (Feels like they just pressed the exit button.)
- If there is anything you need, just ask. (Appreciated, but often hard for us to ask.)
- I can't be with you, but I am sending you a care package. (Much appreciated.)
- I'm coming over, and I'm bringing a meal. (Very much appreciated.)
- Don't worry. God has a plan for everything. (This is not helpful—and not true.)
- My aunt also had cancer; it was terrible. (Horror stories are better not shared.)
- Having cancer will give you more time to pray. (Maybe true, but not necessarily helpful. What do you think we've been doing?!)
- God wants to get your attention. (Couldn't God have figured out another way?)
- Are you going to have reconstruction? My sister didn't and her husband left her. (Downer.)

Insights from Our Journey with Cancer

When in crisis, keeping secrets is not a sign of strength. I think deep inside we knew that, but for many of us that's our default mode, especially when dealing with the dreaded C word. I know it was for me. In some strange way, there was a hidden hope that if I didn't talk about the illness, it would somehow take care of itself and simply go away. I wish it would have, but life doesn't work that way.

It was healing to let others know what we were dealing with, giving them the opportunity to step in and share the journey. In hindsight, it was not selfish to do so. We found that even the smallest acts of kindness—a bouquet of flowers, a plate of cookies, some new pajamas, or a handwritten card—were deeply meaningful, bringing a ray of light to an otherwise dark time. As humbling as it was to ask for help and as difficult as it was to accept it gracefully when it came, we were better for it. Some unexpected people stepped up in unexpected ways. I think of it as an unexpected means of grace.

Waiting was really hard, especially waiting for days for the test results to come in or sitting alone in a hushed hospital waiting room for news about yet another examination or the success of the surgery. It was difficult to find any joy in such times—and very tiring too. Waiting by yourself for hours at a time while dealing with such uncertainty can be downright painful and isolating. I don't recommend it. And the resulting onslaught of bills wasn't that much fun either.

Along the way, we received some unwanted advice and were offered some downright strange spiritual explanations for the cancer. Although well meaning, such "words of comfort" came across as insensitive and even hurtful at times. Try not to dwell on them.

Looking back, we came to appreciate the advances in medicine and the expertise and dedication of care providers. We had no idea how much medical skill, knowledge, and compassion was available to us in our own hometown. It was an unexpected blessing. And we came away with an entirely new perspective and sensitivity to others with cancer and other types of traumas. We pray that we will always have eyes to see and ears to hear, to be witnesses with those who suffer or spend days in the waiting room.

TAKEAWAYS ABOUT FLOODS FOR ALL OF US

Floods Do Come

None of us are immune from the floods of life. Some we create, most just find us along the way, but all of them change everything instantly. The worries and to-do list for that day become irrelevant. The focus of each day is diagnosis, treatment, and recovery. It can be overwhelming, and depressing at times too, but in the midst of it all, there are also times of deep contentment and evergreen hope. It doesn't always make sense and can't be easily explained, but I know it's true. I've been there when it happened. It is simply a mystery to embrace and be thankful when it comes your way.

Floods bring trauma to your front door, an uninvited but persistent visitor. They don't just disappear on their own. It takes resolve and support. And along with the trauma comes a deep sense of loss. We may lose our property, a job, our health, a loved one, our marriage, our social standing, our friends, our identity, our sense of well-being, even our faith. Sometimes the trauma is hidden by the first visible losses of the flood, but it will revisit us again and again if we don't face it. Trauma can't be ignored or covered up with a fresh coat of paint.

Arks and Life Rafts

It's too late to build an ark when the forty days and nights of rain come. Of course, floods can rarely be anticipated, but it is possible to build an ark to carry you through a crisis by the way you live your life. In particular, care for your body, mind, and spirit through daily practices that develop and deepen your sense of well-being; good insurance, regular savings, a life lived simply, a vital network of friends and family, a truth teller who loves you, and a life-giving faith community are ways to build an ark before the forty days of rain come your way.

It is equally important to be mindful that we can and do play a key role in the construction of other arks. We can cultivate deep friendships and lend support, food, encouragement, prayer, and presence in good times and bad. For those of us who have been through a flood or two ourselves, we understand the toll it takes to stay afloat. Connecting and reaching out to others without invitation ought to be second nature. Rather than expecting someone in need to ask for help, just act—do something, anything! After all, they *are* in need; we all are. God, give us eyes to see and ears to hear.

And if we don't have an ark or the floods sweep away our safety net, we must cobble together a life raft as best we can. We are in panic mode, casting here and there for any kind of assistance, kindness, and relief we can find—sometimes just a blanket and a hot meal or a hug—anything! I find it amazing that in the depth of our darkest hours and our deepest need, people we don't even know show up time and time again, offering more than we could ever imagine. In the aftermath of a flood, the best of community and church shows itself. Getting the life raft to shore is a communal act, full of grace.

Starting Over

Floods do recede, but they leave a high-water mark. Long after the signs of the flood are gone or covered over, there is still the trauma, loss, and memory to deal with. I have come to believe that recovery is not a solo race, and it is certainly not a sprint. In fact, it is not a race at all. Recovery is more of a group hike up a long and steep hill, best conquered with time, care, one or two deep friendships, professional expertise of many different kinds, a vibrant faith community, courage, and grit. I mention one or two deep friendships simply because that's about all you can count on in a flood. Sadly, many "friends" simply fade away when we're in crisis. I don't really know why, but I know they do.

Starting over is never easy. Sometimes you wonder if it is worth the effort to even try to put things back like they were. Sometimes you can't; there is no "back like things were" to go back to. This can be painful, but it can also be a time to try something new, to make a move, to find a new job, to develop a new set of relationships, or nurture a new sense of direction. Remember, when the Bible speaks of forty days and forty nights, it is usually a time of hardship and trials, but it can also be a time of transition and a fresh start. No one wants to be hit by a flood, but sometimes we can look back and see God's fingerprints all over our hardships—with us before the flood, in the ark or on the life raft, with us today, and when we get to where we are headed, to wherever "there" is, God is already there and working on our behalf, bringing grace, healing, and hope.

God's Promise

God promised Noah, "As long as the earth endures, seedtime and harvest, cold and heat, summer and winter, day and night will never cease" (Gen 8:22). That's a promise for all of us. After the flood, life will go on. Providence will rise before the sun.

Of course, there may be pain, sorrow, discouragement, and a sense of loss. Floods do that. They take things from you. And healing takes time, sometimes a lifetime, but we are never left alone to make our own way. And when we see a rainbow, it's a good time to whisper a prayer of thanks for all the blessings in our lives, known and unknown, remembered and forgotten. Floods will come and go, but God will always be present.

CLOSING COMMENTS

The first eleven chapters of Genesis are best thought of as humanity's attempt over a number of centuries to understand and explain God's desire to be in relationship with us. Although we, all of us, are made in God's image, we continue to come up short time after time after time. We always have, and yet God persists.

So, I believe that Genesis is best understood as theology, not history, and the story of Noah is part of that collective theology. It is important to keep our focus on what the story of Noah is trying to tell us about a God who desires to be in relationship with us. The Bible tells us of the many ways God has tried to get our attention through covenants, correction, prophets, priests, kings, and sometimes floods, giants, and whales, all with limited success. I wonder if God finally thought, "Next time, I'll come myself." What I do know is this: God did.

CHAPTER FOUR

Despair—Elijah

Then the word of the Lord came to him, saying, "What are you doing here, Elijah?"

—I KGS 19:9B

INTRODUCTION

THE STORIES OF THE great prophet Elijah circulated among the Hebrew people long before they were compiled and written down. He was a true hero of the people, famous for his battle with the four hundred and fifty prophets of Baal on Mount Carmel, and for his meeting with God on Mount Horeb. And centuries after being taken up to heaven in a whirlwind, he appeared at Jesus' transfiguration as recorded in all three Synoptic Gospels (Matt 17:3; Mark 9:4; Luke 9:30). Even Paul in his letter to the Romans quoted from Elijah's conversation with the God of the Gentle Whisper on Mount Horeb (11:2–4). A major Old Testament prophet indeed!

And yet, despite achieving prophetic hero status, he did lose his way from time to time, his sense of true north, if you will. At one point, he was even ready to give up, to give it *all* up. In this chapter, we will look at Elijah's triumphs, his shortcomings, and his bout with despair. In particular, we'll follow him on his weary journey of forty days and forty nights through the wilderness to meet God on Mount Horeb, and then another forty-days-and-nights journey as he headed back home to continue his work, albeit after a reality check, an attitude adjustment, and a missional reset. It was a clarification and transition in his calling. I think many of us have made these journeys too, and some of us more than once.

Jeroboam

When Elijah made his first appearance in the Bible (1 Kgs 17), coming seemingly out of nowhere, Ahab was king of Israel. To say the least, he was not a good king, and he followed a litany of terrible kings—Jeroboam, Nadab, Baasha, Elah, Zimri, and Omri (Ahab's father). The Bible tells us that each succeeding king was as bad as, if not worse than, the previous one. They seemed to be competing for the "most unfaithful king" award, each trying in their own way to outdo the evil works of Jeroboam, Israel's first king after Solomon's kingdom was divided. At the outset, Jeroboam feared that if his people went back to the temple in Jerusalem to offer sacrifices, their allegiance would revert back to King Rehoboam, and that would be the end of him. So, Jeroboam set up two golden calves in his own territory for his people to worship, constructed shrines in high places, instituted their own special religious festivals, and even "appointed priests from all sorts of people, even though they were not Levites" (1 Kgs 13: 33b).

All this was totally unacceptable, so God sent Ahijah the prophet to relay a message: "I raised you up from among the people and appointed you ruler over my people Israel . . . but you have not been like my servant David. . . . You have done more evil than all who lived before you. You have made for yourself other gods, idols made of metal; you have aroused my anger and turned your back on me. . . . Because of this, I am going to bring disaster on the house of Jeroboam as one burns dung, until it is gone" (1 Kgs 14: 7–10).

Now, I don't know about you, but if I received a message from God that my actions were more evil that all who lived before me and my house would be burned like dung, I would be in total panic mode. I would be repenting and pleading with God to give me another chance to make amends and change my ways, but not so with King Jeroboam. He continued to reign for twenty-two years, unchanged, unashamed, and unbowed, and passed this legacy to his successors for six generations until Elijah met up with King Ahab—the worst of the bunch.

Ahab and Jezebel

Why? How could Ahab be even worse than all of his predecessors? We find the answer in 1 Kgs 16: "Ahab son of Omri did more evil in the eyes of the Lord than any of those before him. He not only considered it trivial to commit the sins of Jeroboam son of Nebat, but he also married Jezebel daughter of EthBaal king of the Sidonians, and began to serve Baal and worship him. He set up an altar for Baal in the temple of Baal . . . and made an Asherah pole" (vv. 30–33). So, Scripture tells us that Ahab was the worst king for two reasons. First, he considered it "trivial" to continue the practice of sponsoring a state religion in Israel rather than letting his people go to Jerusalem to offer their sacrifices. Simply put, it was a political strategy to maintain control. It was clearly wrong in God's eyes, but nonetheless effective. It was all about the self-serving use of religion for control.

The second reason was all about water. In those times and in that arid region, no self-respecting king could retain power without water. Rains seemed to come in cycles, and if the king could guarantee water for his people (taking credit when it rained), he would be king indeed. If he couldn't (and couldn't find anyone else to blame), the people would blame him—and he would be toast. It was that simple. That's where his marriage to Jezebel comes in. Ahab was looking for any edge he could find in the water-provision business. He knew that a marriage to someone who worshiped a Phoenician god would not go over well, but Jezebel's god was Baal. This Canaanite god was the god of fertility, and that included the fertility of the land. And how did Baal keep the land fertile? By sending rain. For Ahab, water was power, and the worship of Baal was the edge he needed.

However, even if the worship of Baal was allowed in Israel as a minor hobby of the king, Jezebel took it to an entirely different level. She instituted the worship of Baal as an official alternative to the worship of Yahweh, and worked to eliminate the worship of Yahweh altogether by destroying alters and killing the prophets who served the Lord. This was simply unacceptable, but what could the people of Israel do against the power of the king and his queen? Enter: Elijah the Tishbite.

Elijah the Tishbite

The very first time Elijah makes an appearance in the narrative, or anywhere in the Bible for that matter, we are told this: "Now Elijah the Tishbite, from Tishbe in Gilead, said to Ahab, 'As the Lord, the God of Israel, lives, whom I serve, there will be neither dew nor rain in the next few years except by my word'" (1 Kgs 17:1). That's it. We know almost nothing else about Elijah. How old was he? What was his occupation? How was he raised? What kind of a family did he come from? Who were his mentors and teachers? How religious was he? Where did he come from? And how did he gain an audience with Ahab? Was he living locally, known to the king's aids, or did he somehow catch Ahab's attention while he was out for an afternoon stroll? We just don't know.

We are told that Elijah was a Tishbite, from Tishbe in Gilead, but as it turns out, that doesn't tell us much either. Tishbe could have been his current residence or his birthplace—or neither. Some scholars (serious Biblical scholars often disagree) believe that Tishbe in Gilead could be translated from the original Hebrew as "of the settlers" or "a resident alien," so we don't really know where Elijah was living at the time, where he came from, or why he was in the king's neighborhood.

What we do know is that Elijah told King Ahab that he served the God of Israel, and that unless and until God decided differently, there would be neither dew nor rain for the next few years. The clear message was that Israel's God was in total control of fertility and life, not Baal. That was the message, and Ahab didn't like it a bit. There was little he could do about it, however, and he had to go home and tell his wife, Jezebel. That couldn't have been a pleasant conversation.

Probably for reasons of personal safety, God instructed Elijah to go to a brook in the Kerith Ravine and stay there. It was in the middle of nowhere. Ravens would bring him bread and meat twice a day, and he could drink from the brook. He did as he was instructed, and the ravens came faithfully. He stayed there until the brook went dry. The drought that Elijah predicted was now full on, so God instructed him to travel to the city of Zarephath in the region of Sidon. There he would meet a widow and her son. He was to stay with them and God promised to provide food for the three of them. Elijah did, and God did.

Curiously, after the meeting with Ahab, Elijah hid first by himself in the wilderness, but then traveled to Zarephath, a populous city in the heart of Baal-worship country. Perhaps the best way to go unnoticed is to go about your business in plain sight. At one point, the widow's son became gravely ill and stopped breathing. Elijah prayed a powerful and heartfelt prayer for healing and the boy recovered. When Elijah returned the boy to his mother, the widow exclaimed, "Now I know that you are a man of God and that the word of the Lord from your mouth is the truth" (1 Kgs 17:24). Coming from someone living in the heart of Baal-worship country, that was a powerful testimony, indeed. It would soon be put to the test.

THE CONTEST ON MOUNT CARMEL

Meeting Ahab for the Second Time

After about three years, God instructed Elijah to present himself to King Ahab again and announce that the drought (at God's initiation) would soon be over. On the way, Elijah ran into Obadiah, Ahab's palace administrator but a faithful follower of the Lord, who was out looking for any water and green grass that might still be found to feed the king's mules and horses. Obadiah was thrilled to see Elijah, and told him how, while Jezebel was hunting and killing the Lord's prophets, he managed to hide one hundred prophets of the Lord in caves, thus saving their lives. However, when Elijah told him to go back and tell Ahab that he wanted to talk with him, Obadiah panicked and asked, "What have I done wrong . . . that you are handing your servant over to Ahab to be put to death?" (1 Kgs 18:9). He told Elijah that his king had been leading a manhunt for him for some time, even in adjoining nations and kingdoms. Obadiah feared that if he told the king that Elijah was here to see him and Elijah would suddenly disappear again, he would be left holding the bag. Elijah promised that he wouldn't do that to him, and he didn't.

When Ahab finally met up with Elijah face-to-face, he yelled, "Is that you, you troubler of Israel?" (I Kgs 18:17). Elijah fired back that it was not he, but the king and the king's father's family who were the culprits, abandoning the Lord's commands and following Baal. It must have been tense, a standoff of sorts, but what happened next came totally out of the blue. Elijah looked the king squarely in the eyes and said, "Now summon the people from all over Israel to meet me on Mount Carmel. And bring the four hundred and fifty prophets of Baal and the four hundred prophets of Asherah, who eat at Jezebel's table" (1 Kgs 18:19). Ahab agreed. It was game on!

(As a side note, the four hundred prophets of Asherah are never mentioned again in the story of Elijah. Maybe Jezebel wouldn't let them come to Mount Carmel; maybe they were afraid to take part in the contest; maybe they were disinterested; or maybe they . . . we really don't know.)

A Contest Is Proposed

Ahab sent a message throughout Israel to meet him on Mount Carmel. It must have been a big event—like the state fair without the rides. Elijah confronted the people and asked how long they would go on worshiping with split allegiances. They responded with silence. Then Elijah proposed a contest between himself (he characterized himself as the only one of the Lord's prophets left alive, apparently forgetting the one hundred prophets that Obadiah saved) and the four hundred and fifty prophets of Baal. They would set up an offering and see which god would answer by fire. This time the people responded, "What you say is good" (1 Kgs 18:24b). Game on, indeed!

The prophets of Baal chose a bull, set up an altar, and tried all day to call down fire. They shouted, danced, sang, cut themselves with spears and swords, and even tried prophesizing a time or two, all to no avail. Elijah engaged in a good bit of taunting too, sounding like an obnoxious Knicks fan taunting the opposition at a game in Madison Square Garden. Then, when it was time for the evening sacrifice, Elijah rebuilt the altar of the Lord using twelve stones, one for each of Jacob's tribes, dug a trench around the altar, arranged the wood, cut up a bull, placed the pieces on the alter, and then as a final measure, he had the people bring in jars of water to saturate the entire sacrificial platform until even the trench was overflowing. All was ready.

Elijah prayed a simple prayer imploring God to send fire. It would be a sign to all, he said, that the God of the Israelites was the only true God. Instantly fire fell from above, consuming everything—the sacrifice, the altar, the wood, the stones, the water, even the soil. The people were convinced and, at Elijah's direction, they rounded up all the prophets of Baal, took them down to the Kishon Valley, and slaughtered them. It must have been horrific to witness.

While all this was going on, Elijah told King Ahab to celebrate because the rains were on the way just as God said, but he should take care to head down the mountain and back to Jezreel while the roads were passable. Ahab followed Elijah's instructions and rode off. Just then, the power of the Lord came on Elijah, we are told. He tucked in his cloak and ran ahead of Ahab all the way back to Jezreel, a distance of about seventeen miles!

What a great day for the God of Israel, the only true God, and what a great day for Elijah too, the only true prophet left (or so he thought). He was running back to Jezreel to be greeted as a hero. What could possibly go wrong?

IN THE WILDERNESS

In a word, what went wrong was—Jezebel. We're not entirely sure what Ahab thought would happen that day on Mount Carmel, but we do know that when he told Jezebel how Elijah won the contest and how he had all the prophets of Baal killed, Jezebel went ballistic. She promised that Elijah would be dead within twenty-four hours. And how did the winner of the mountaintop contest, the hero of the people and the faithful servant of the Lord respond? "Elijah was afraid and ran for his life" (1 Kgs 19:3). He fled!

He first traveled out of Ahab's jurisdiction, which was probably a good idea, and then walked a day's journey into the wilderness. There, he sat under a broom bush and prayed that he might die, feeling like he was no better than any of his ancestors. What a sudden reversal of circumstance and emotion. In less than a day, he went from being a winner to a loser, from a prophetic hero to a fugitive, from total euphoria to abject despair. How could this be?

In Despair

Actually, it's not uncommon to experience a major letdown right after a mountaintop experience of any kind. After all, it's not healthy or even possible to survive long term in such thin air, although we would love to do so. We have to come down the mountain sooner or later. Real life beckons us. Sometimes the way back down is a slow, deliberate descent, and at other times, like Elijah's, it is a free fall. Why?

In Elijah's case, there are three likely possibilities for his emotional crash after such a major success, and they may be related. First, there's exhaustion or—even though the word wasn't familiar to the Hebrews—burnout. He was so busy working for the Lord that he went over the top, way over the top. Think about it. The

Lord told Elijah to go to Ahab and tell him that rain would be coming. That was the entire message. And he did, but he also told Ahab to summon people from all over Israel to come to Mount Carmel for a major event. That was Elijah's doing. Nor did the Lord instruct Elijah to challenge all four hundred and fifty prophets of Baal to a fire-calling contest. He did that all on his own. The Lord didn't tell him to convert the sacrificial altar into a big demonstration stage, and no one told Elijah to dig a trench around the altar and fill it with water. Remember, it hadn't rained for three years, so water was one of the people's most precious commodities, a life-giving necessity. That was Elijah grandstanding on his own, not at the instruction of the Lord.

And the Lord didn't instruct Elijah to publicly taunt and ridicule his opponents or go on a half-marathon victory run in front of Ahab's horse all the way back to Jezreel. He did all of this on his own too, and he wore himself out in the process! I'm sure that he thought that he was doing everything he could to help the Lord win the day, to do the Lord's bidding, but in the end he simply ran out of gas—he was totally spent. An emotional crash was predictable. You can't help wondering if it wasn't more about promoting himself than helping God all along, even though I'm sure it never even crossed his mind. I've done the same thing myself.

In addition to suffering from burnout, it is quite possible that he was caught totally off guard by Jezebel's promise to kill him. He didn't see that response coming, expecting instead to be received as the hero in a big parade held in his honor. It must have hit him full in the face, leaving him feeling vulnerable and defenseless. So, he ran away, fearing his life was over. It's a natural reaction to such an unexpected threat, especially when your physical and emotional resources are spent. And when you are at the end of your rope, despair is a frequent companion.

I remember one Saturday when I was twelve. My father was out for the day, so I decided that I would surprise him by cleaning and organizing our garage, or to be more precise, *his* garage. I worked on the project most of the day, and although I was exhausted, I was feeling a very deep sense of pride when my dad's pickup pulled into the driveway that evening. I just wanted to please him. I stood in front of the open doorway with a big grin on my face, broom in hand. Without any expression he looked around a bit, pointed out some places that he thought I missed, and grumbled that he wouldn't be able to find anything since some of his tools were in a new place. As he turned and walked into the house, I turned and ran to the backyard with tears streaming down my face. In a real sense, my spirit was broken. Instead of recognition and gratitude, I received a sour dose of criticism. It wasn't at all what I expected. I never tried to clean out that damn garage again. I can only imagine the magnitude of Elijah's disappointment and despair when the hero's welcome he'd expected didn't manifest itself, but instead the reality that his life was in jeopardy did. It wasn't what he expected. His victory didn't eliminate the competition, and it didn't end the battle with Baal. Afraid for his life, he fled.

There is a third possibility, and we don't talk about it much in church. After the victory over the prophets of Baal, Elijah commanded the people to seize the prophets and take them to the Kishon Valley. There they were slaughtered—all four hundred and fifty of them. Simply put, it was a massacre. One has to wonder if that was really what God wanted to happen. Was there not another solution? They could have been sent back to their home country, or into exile somewhere, or jailed, but slaughtered? Could it be that in addition to being afraid and over the top, Elijah was also out of line—way out of line, and as the euphoria of the day began to wear off, remorse began to set in that night about all the violence he had encouraged that day? Could it be that that is what Elijah meant when he wailed that he was no better than his ancestors? Honestly, we don't know, but it is a real possibility.

Quite likely, it is some combination of the three possibilities, and it left Elijah sitting under a broom bush wishing to die, in deep despair, but that's not the end of the story. He didn't know it, but he was about to be sent on a journey, a journey of forty days and forty nights. It was perhaps the most important journey of his life, a passage preparing him for a major reset.

FORTY DAYS AND FORTY NIGHTS

Elijah found some cover under a broom bush and went to sleep. God could have immediately confronted this wayward prophet about showing off and wearing himself out, about his out-of-line offences, and his running away right there on the spot. Why not address the problem immediately, head-on? That's what I would have done, but that isn't what happened. First, an angel brought him some fresh-baked bread and water, woke him up, and told him to get up and eat. He did, but then went right back to sleep. The angel came a second time, instructing him to eat and drink in preparation for a journey to Mount Horeb. It would take him forty days and forty nights. Why the long journey?

The forty days and nights would give Elijah space to prepare for a meeting with God, and in his condition, he surely needed it! He would be asked some very hard questions about his conduct, but, at the time, he wasn't able to even hear the questions, let alone respond in any healthy way. After a crisis event we often seclude ourselves too, eating the wrong things or refusing to eat at all, staying up late and watching TV, laying on the couch with the blinds pulled, and refusing to even go out for the mail. In hindsight, they are the wrong things to do, but when you're in despair, sleeping under a broom bush feels so right.

Perhaps Elijah didn't fully understand it, but the forty-days-and-nights journey would give him three things he sorely needed to ready himself to face the reality of his situation: daily exercise, time to reflect, and something to look forward to (a trip to Mount Horeb). Together, they provided space for some serious interior work. When Elijah finally arrived on Mount Horeb, he found a cave and spent the night. He was ready to meet God—or so he thought.

ON MOUNT HOREB

In the morning, the word of the Lord came to Elijah in the form of an existential question: "What are you doing here, Elijah?" (1 Kgs 19:9b). He started rambling through the same old speech he gave while sitting under the broom bush about being zealous and faithful for the Lord although all the Israelites had rejected the covenant, all the prophets of the Lord were dead, and he was the only one left—not remembering or "choosing to forget" what Obadiah told him about the one hundred prophets that he personally saved during Jezebel's latest crusade. Apparently, the forty days and nights journey didn't change Elijah's perspective all that much. Old narratives are hard to break.

The Lord instructed Elijah to go outside and stand in the presence of the Lord. He did, and what an experience it must have been! There was a wind so powerful that it shattered rocks, then an earthquake, and then fire, just the way Elijah thought that God would and should show up, but God was not in them. This was a not-so-subtle theological lesson for Elijah about the nature of God. Not everything was about strength, power, and destruction. Sometimes God could be heard in the sound of sheer silence. Perhaps that was the way the Lord's prophets should act too. Not everything was about power, confrontation, and destruction.

As it turned out, God did come in a gentle whisper, and repeated the question: What are you doing here, Elijah? He started through his well-rehearsed speech, but this time God said, in effect, "Enough! Go back the way you came, appoint Hazael king over Aram, Jehu as king over Israel, and Elisha as your successor!! You need a major reset. This work is not about you, and you need to get some help. There is plenty available if you only have eyes to see and the humility to take advantage of it. Oh, and by the way, there are seven thousand in Israel who have not bowed down to Baal. You are not and never have been the only one left who worships me and keeps the covenant. Don't kid yourself. End of discussion."

So, Elijah made the return trip to the desert of Damascus, another forty days and forty nights, a true time of transition. I'm sure he had much to think about on the way. Although he didn't anoint Hazael and Jehu as kings (Elisha later did), he did find Elisha and took him on as his understudy and companion. Elijah continued his prophetic work, but with a reality check, an attitude adjustment, and a missional reset. The work wasn't all about him. From time to time, I think we all need to hear that message too. It's never all about us.

CLOSING COMMENTS

I'm sure that Elisha knew about Elijah's exploits on Mount Carmel, but I wonder if Elijah ever told him about his conversation with God on Mount Horeb and his two journeys of forty days and forty nights, one journey leading to an attitude adjustment and a reality check, and the other leading to a major missional reset. What he understood about God and what he understood about his own role as a prophet would never be the same. To share such a transition would take humility and courage. I hope he did, but I don't really know.

What I do know is this: When it was clear that Elijah was in his very last days, he asked Elisha what he could do for him before he was taken. Elisha replied, "Let me have a double portion of your spirit" (2 Kgs 2:9b). Clearly, Elisha saw something in Elijah's spirit that he not only wanted to have, but he wanted to have it twofold! I can't help but think that his two journeys of forty days and nights had something to do with the renewal of his spirit. He experienced grace, rest, and renewal during one of the darkest times of his life. When we experience our own times of despair as a result of fear, burnout, or foolish actions, may we journey to the mountain and back again too. We can count on this: life is messy, but God is faithful.

CHAPTER FIVE

Silence—Ezekiel

After you have finished this, lie down again, this time on your right side, and bear the sin of the people. I have assigned you forty days, a day for each year.

—EZEK 4:6

INTRODUCTION

IN THIS BOOK, WE have thus far examined events in the lives of Moses, David, Noah, and Elijah where forty days and forty nights came into play: times of profound disappointment, battles with giants, facing overwhelming floods, and dealing with deep despair. You will remember that the phrase "forty days and forty nights" can refer to hard times of suffering, hardship, testing, and trial, but also to times of change, challenge, and transition. They all experienced both.

This is a unique chapter. We will meet a devout priest, Ezekiel, who was called to be a prophet among his own people by a series of strange divine visions in a most unusual place—Babylonian exile. It is a story of the faithful work of a forceful truth teller, sometimes appreciated and sometimes not so much. Being a priest and a prophet at the same time is never an easy balancing act, but as it turns out, Ezekiel was up to the challenge. Along with his warnings, condemnations, oracles, sign acts, and chilling prophecies, he offered words of hope to those who were in exile with him—the promise of a new heart, a renewed spirit, and a restored home for the faithful remanent.

After a look at the life and times of the prophet along with the Old Testament book that bears his name, we will discuss several activities from the book that I believe we can appropriate to deepen our own spiritual journeys: living in exile, being both priest and prophet, having visions, using sign acts, challenging faulty theology, and offering hope. Forty days and nights come to all of us in many different ways, and what Ezekiel experienced may be the most challenging of all. He was instructed by God to prophesy to his people, but to be silent, to say nothing for forty days and forty nights unless God instructed him otherwise. For any prophet, that is certainly not the preferred mode of communication, but Ezekiel did as he was instructed. We'll see how he did it.

The Prophet Ezekiel

We don't know much about Ezekiel's life before he was called to be a prophet while in exile in Babylon at age thirty, the first to be recognized as a prophet outside of Judah and Israel. We do know that he lived in Jerusalem and served as a priest along with his father, Buzi, who claimed a priestly lineage. He was following in the family business.

In 597 BCE Ezekiel was deported to Babylon along with about ten thousand of his fellow citizens after King Jehoiachin led a failed revolt in Jerusalem. He was twenty-five when he arrived in Babylon. According to the Bible, Ezekiel and his wife lived there in their own house on the banks of the Kebar Canal in an exiled Judean community. There is no mention of any children.

He was serving as a priest when he was commissioned by God to a new, dramatic, and daunting role: "And you, son of man, do not be afraid of them or their words. Do not be afraid, though briers and thorns are all around you and you live among scorpions.

... You must speak my words to them, whether they listen or fail to listen, for they are a rebellious house" (Ezek 2:6-7). The "them" that God was referring to was *his own community in exile*. Ezekiel was to prophesy and warn the exiled Judaeans, not their Babylonian captors. A daunting task, indeed, but one that he carried out faithfully for over two decades.

The Book of Ezekiel

Ezekiel is one of the most fascinating books in the Bible, but also one of the most confusing, misunderstood, and misused. Some Christian traditions have embraced Ezekiel's visions as being deeply profound and relevant for our lives today, so they work diligently to mine the visions and prophecies to decode their hidden meaning, messages sent to only a select few. Other traditions have virtually ignored the book—except for the valley of dry bones vision, a standard preaching go-to when urging for renewal in the church or offering a hopeful example that renewal can happen in the most unlikely of places. Some Jewish religious leaders even considered it too dangerous to be read in group settings of any kind or by individuals under the age of thirty.

Ezekiel is referenced often in the book of Revelation but virtually ignored in the rest of the New Testament. You can make of that what you will. I do suggest that you read the book in its entirety, along with a reliable commentary or two. Understanding the nature, scope, context, and organization of the book is certainly worth the effort, but trying to decode Ezekiel's visions for hidden meaning and secret communications from God to a modern-day prophet, I don't recommend (my personal view).

The book of Ezekiel is anchored by six extraordinary visions told in detail by Ezekiel, that, along with his prophecies and symbolic performances (sign acts), call the exiles to accountability for their malpractice in worship. They also foretell the fall of Jerusalem, the destruction of the temple, condemnation of all Judah, and judgment of Judah's neighbors and adversaries as well. Along the way, however, Ezekiel holds out hope that a faithful remnant from exile will eventually return to rebuild the temple and the city, enlivened by a new heart in a renewed land. It is an enduring message of hope, accompanied by a necessary theological correction. Clearly, while prophesying and calling his fellow exiles to accountability for idol worship (among other things), Ezekiel never lost his priestly heart for his people. As I read it, this is the abiding message of the book that bears his name, and a lesson for all of us who take our worship seriously and care for those who worship with us.

Forty Days and Nights

Before we highlight and examine six significant activities in the life of Ezekiel that I believe have much to speak to us today, I want to say just a word about the forty days and nights mentioned in this chapter. We have witnessed Moses climbing and staying on Mount Sinai for forty days and nights—twice; Goliath walking out and issuing a challenge to Saul's army forty days and nights in a row; Noah watching torrents of rain fall for forty days and nights before the flood brought the ark into play; and Elijah traveling forty days and nights to Horeb, the mountain of God, and then forty days and nights back home again. Ezekiel's forty-day experience was different.

Ezekiel's forty days and nights were not spent heading up a mountain or waiting for a flood to arrive or a fight to break out. Instead, he was to construct a model of the city of Jerusalem under siege, complete with ramps, battering rams, and enemy camps surrounding the city. Then, he was to lie on his right side, bare his arms as a sign of war, and stare at the model and the people who came by—and *say nothing* unless specifically instructed by God to do so. A different way to spend forty days to be sure!

In addition, in many ways Ezekiel's forty days and nights on his right side was not an isolated event or even the central event, but simply part of a much larger demonstration prophecy predicting the fall of Jerusalem. It followed a longer period of days (390, we are told) lying on his left side, along with a demonstration of the food rationing that would occur during the siege. It was certainly a hardship, but it wasn't a time of great personal transition for him.

Still, these forty days are important. They demonstrate Ezekiel's obedience in the face of anger, disbelief, rumor, and ridicule. It couldn't have been easy. It wasn't a popular message to deliver, but he didn't argue, start a fight, or give the onlookers a piece of his mind, although I imagine that he was tempted to do so a time or two. He just did what he was called to do—and kept his mouth shut the rest of the time. There's a lesson in this story for all of us.

Before we close this chapter by looking at several activities found in the book of Ezekiel that I believe have particular relevance for our own spiritual formation, let me say just a word about the forty nights. We really don't know what Ezekiel did each night, but most scholars presume that at sunset he went back home. Did he come in the front door and announce, "I'm home! What's for dinner?" We don't know. What did his wife think about his visions, prophecies, condemnations, and daily activities in the public square? We don't know that either, but it is fun to speculate. What we do know is that Ezekiel showed up morning after morning after morning, faithfully doing what he was supposed to do. God promised to give him a forehead "like the hardest stone, harder than flint" (Ezek 2:9a). I'm sure he needed it.

WHAT CAN WE LEARN FROM EZEKIEL

Living in Exile

To be in exile is to be barred, removed, or situated away from one's own country, culture, community, or religion, and usually with limited economic and social mobility. Living in exile is never easy, even if done so by choice or for high purpose. In essence, it requires living without roots or wings, to be cut off, to be untethered from one's home community and unable to leave or move up or move on without paying a high personal price of one kind or another. And it can be a time of spiritual transition too, whether it is recognized at the time or not.

Exile is one of the major themes of the Bible, particularly in the Old Testament. Adam and Eve were banished from Eden (Gen 3:23–24). After killing his brother, Cain was driven from his land, becoming "a restless wanderer on the earth" (Gen 3:12b). The great flood washed away Noah's home and community, requiring him to start over in a new place not of his own choosing (Gen 6–10). The writer of Hebrews tells us that "by faith Abraham, when called to go to a place he would later receive as his inheritance, obeyed and went . . . he made his home in the promised land *like a stranger in a foreign country*" (Heb 11:8–9; italics mine). And Moses was an exile his entire life. He died looking over the promised land from a high mountain perch, but never made it across the river to build a home there (Deut 3:27).

Two mass exiles in the Old Testament bear mentioning. After King Solomon's death, the kingdom that was united by his father, David, split: Israel to the north representing ten of the original tribes of Israel, and Judah to the south with the remaining two tribes and the city of Jerusalem. Both were subjected to mass deportations by invading kingdoms. Over 150 years before Ezekiel, the Assyrians occupied most of Israel and sent thousands into exile. Known as the Assyrian Exile or Assyrian Captivity, it came in waves over several decades and was carefully planned and orchestrated by the Assyrian government. The purpose was to gain new territory for resettlement, to acquire workers for low-level agricultural and project work at home, to enrich the Assyrian culture with highly skilled artists, doctors, teachers, and technicians from Israel, and to punish and destroy opposition to Assyrian rule. Returning home for those in exile was entirely out of the question.

The end goal was to totally eradicate Israel's culture and identity. The Assyrians worked intentionally to eliminate all aspects of the exiles' former religious activities, their social networks, their families, and their communal identity. The Israelites were not allowed to practice their own religion. Instead, they were forced to worship Assyrian gods. Communities and existing family units were disbanded; intermarriage was required. The Assyrian assimilation was so successful that the kingdom of Israel never recovered, and the ten tribes gradually disappeared from history.

Ezekiel was part of the Babylonian exile. In some ways it was an easier kind of exile to endure. They were allowed to practice their own religion and live together in segregated populations. Ezekiel and others lived in their own homes and were able to conduct religious services there. When the Judaeans were allowed to return to Jerusalem, many decided to stay in Babylon, offering evidence to some historians that the Babylonian exile was just as good as being home. However, when you read Ps 137, it is easy to hear the pain of exile: "By the rivers of Babylon we sat and wept when we remembered Zion. There on the poplars we hung our harps, . . . our tormentors demanded songs of joy; they said, 'Sing' . . . [but] how can we sing the songs of the Lord while in a foreign land? . . . Daughter Babylon . . . happy is the one who repays you according to what you have done to us. Happy is the one who seizes your infants and dashes them against the rocks" (vv. 1–9). That doesn't sound like a happy exile to me.

Obviously, an Assyrian-style exile is so terrible because it takes away one's agency, personal identity, social, religious, and cultural context, and any hope of returning home. Much of who you are simply disappears. That being said, any form of exile demands a personal price of one kind or another. So, what about us? Few of us will ever face an Assyrian exile, but many of us will find ourselves in an exile of one kind or another. When I informed my boss in late November that I had accepted a new position at another university starting the next July, he immediately demanded my keys, computer, and phone. He assured me that I would be paid the rest of my contract, but I was not to come on campus or attend any university events, and, with the exception of two or three individuals, I became instantly invisible on campus and at our local church. My wife and I were in exile. It wasn't an Assyrian exile, but painful nonetheless.

Several years later, we were still struggling to find a church home when we were invited to help start a church plant in a neighboring community. We jumped at the opportunity and jumped in—totally! We were all in. Work at the church consumed our lives. After four years, although we were doing all we knew to do, it became obvious that our vision for church practice, worship style, community engagement, and our theology of inclusion were incompatible with the pastor's vision. We needed to leave, and I believe the pastor was glad when we did. It was the right decision at the right time, but we found ourselves in exile again. Like Abraham, we were trying our best to be obedient, but we didn't know where we were going or how to know when we got there, wherever "there" was.

So, what do we do when we're in exile? First, we keep the faith—faith in God, of course, faith in a God who is present and loves us unconditionally, but faith in ourselves too. While it is necessary to see our own part in any exile we experience, it is easy to start believing that we are a total failure or that it is all our fault. God is for some reason punishing us. Don't go there. It isn't helpful—and it isn't true.

Second, in the midst of exile, keep hope alive. This is not meant as a slick political mantra, although you could do worse, but rather a spiritual necessity. If faith sets us on a spiritual journey, and I think it does, it is hope that keeps us going, the fuel that powers our daily steps. Without hope, we are simply stuck in the dark, afraid to take the next step. But with hope, we keep our eyes on the horizon for any ray of light or the slightest movement, and we move toward it as an invitation when we see it.

Hope is found as we notice God's presence in our daily lives, in small and simple ways—the smile from a stranger, the joy of a child at play, a note from a friend, a freshly brewed cup of coffee, a good night's sleep, an encouraging conversation with a neighbor, a thoughtful sermon, or a beautiful hymn. They are all small things, but we celebrate them because God is in them—and because there aren't many big miraculous things to recognize and celebrate in times of exile. If they come, be thankful and celebrate, but don't overlook or undervalue the small stuff, the stuff of hope in our everyday lives.

Finally, if faith sends us on a journey and hope keeps us going, it is love that brings us home—either back home or to a home in a new place, out of exile. "Love the Lord your God with all your heart and with all your soul and with all your mind. This is the first and greatest commandment," Jesus tells the expert in the law. "And the second is like it: 'Love your neighbor as yourself.' All the Law and the Prophets hang on these two commandments" (Matt 22:37–40). I believe that most of us have been raised with a sense of how to love God, at least some of the time, but we are not as good at loving our neighbors or ourselves for that matter. Yet, there it is. Jesus says that *all* the Law and the Prophets hang on our ability to do so. We are to love our way out of exile—to find home.

Let me offer just one example. I live in wine country. In this neck of the woods, about 25 percent of the population is Hispanic, providing the necessary work force for the labor intensive care of the vineyards along with other field crops. I was told by a neighbor recently that the Hispanic population in our town is really OK: "They stay to themselves, and I don't see them much except out in the fields." I was troubled by this statement for two reasons. First, the statement felt dismissive and objectifying. "They" felt a good deal like "us and them," and that does not build a healthy community of any sustainable kind.

The second reason is that it hit me that the field workers in my own town are living in a Babylonian exile of sorts, perhaps by their own choosing (if they had a real choice), but Babylonian exile, nonetheless. If I am to love my neighbors as myself, I must be concerned with issues of justice, equality, and safety. If not, Babylonian exile can too easily slip into Assyrian exile. Of course, to love our neighbors as ourselves asks more of us than just to ensure justice for all, but it is a very good place to start. I will leave it up to each of us to think prayerfully about our neighbors in exile of any kind and find ways to love them dearly—and the ones who live next door too. When we do, we begin to love our way out of our own exile and find our way home.

Being Prophet and Priest

Ezekiel was a priest before he was called to be a prophet among the exiles in Babylon. In a general sense, the two roles were different in several important ways. Priests claimed a priestly lineage and entered their profession as a family responsibility; prophets were singly called by God. Priests provided prayers and rituals leading to forgiveness; prophets communicated instruction, correction, and condemnation. Priests generally worked among the people in the temple or at other religious sites; prophets came literally from anywhere, out of the blue, and left again. Both were mediators: priests brought humanity's requests for forgiveness and goodwill to God; prophets brought God's words of correction and judgment to humanity in a number of unique ways. Priests were organizational, working to keep things running smoothly, providing both process and order; prophets worked as "warners," hoping to unsettle, to bring change. And generally, priests attended to acts of mercy; prophets focused on acts of justice.

Of course, these are generalizations, and while you can quibble with some of the distinctions, I hope you get my point. The two roles were different. Both priests and prophets were required in Israel to sustain meaningful worship, to guide spiritual practices, and to encourage an appropriate understanding of God (theology). The exiles in Babylon needed them too. And so do we—in our own faith community.

(I trust that most of the readers of this book are actively involved in a faith community of some kind. If not, I ask that you consider doing so as the next step in your personal spiritual pilgrimage. I truly believe that we are meant to journey and grow together, particularly when the forty days and nights come our way—and they surely will.)

In our local faith communities, we all have a priestly role to play, to keep things running smoothly and on point. The local church simply cannot fulfill its mission without volunteers: teachers, ushers, sound engineers, worship planners, board members, missions coordinators, gardeners, mowers, landscapers, small group leaders, food bank helpers, etc. There are many more, of course, and those who volunteer for such activities are fulfilling a priestly role just as much as the senior pastor and paid staff. Without priests, the local congregation loses rhythm, structure, and a sense of continuity that provides community, sanctuary, and opportunities for spiritual reflection and engagement each week.

From time to time, we may be called to be a prophet too. In my view, this is always dicey business. Words of caution, correction, or condemnation are rarely invited and seldom appreciated. Knowing when to speak, where to speak, how to speak, and most importantly *when not to speak* requires honest and thoughtful spiritual discernment, and such a role should never be taken lightly or with any sense of entitlement. The Lord told Ezekiel that he would be given a message to share from time to time, and he had a spiritual obligation to speak those words of truth. Beyond that, however, he was to go back to his house and be silent (Ezek 3:26). It wasn't a time to share his own personal opinions or use the occasion to demonstrate his own spiritual superiority or maturity.

The prophetic witness requires courage, prudence, wisdom, and a good dose of humility too. Let me give you a brief example. I was serving on a special project committee at my local church. The project was already underway when I was invited to join the team. As the work went forward, I came to believe that the project was too complex. We were trying to do too much in too little space and time, and it was simply slowing down the project and could lead to other problems down the road.

My solution was to take a step back and simplify the project design before moving forward. At the end of one committee meeting, I took a deep breath and shared my take on the project. It was met with silence. Several meetings later, I tried again with the same result. Finally, I asked the committee a third time to take a moment, hear my concerns, and take them seriously. I shared what I believed to be the problem, and it was cautiously discussed—and then dismissed. The project would go on as planned; there was no mention of my concerns in the minutes.

So, what to do? The Lord told Ezekiel that at the appropriate time, he was to speak. I felt that I needed to speak up too, and I did. The Lord also told Ezekiel that after he spoke, he was to go back to his house and be silent—to go about his business. So, I did that too. Rather than quit the committee and walk away in anger, I decided that I would attend every project committee meeting, stay positive, be engaged, *and say nothing* more about my concerns. I would be silent and help in any way I could. As of this writing, the project continues. I am glad that I spoke up—I needed to—and I'm pleased that the project is moving forward. The outcome will not look exactly as I had envisioned it, and that's ok. Sometimes the best snack for a prophet is a small piece of humble pie.

Seeing Visions

In the book of Ezekiel, the prophet shares six visions: the cherubim (1:4–28), the scroll (2:9–3:3), the plain (3:22–23), Jerusalem (chs. 8–11), dry bones (37:1–28), and the new temple (40:1—48:35). They are an amazing set of visions, and as you might expect, over the centuries they have been regarded in many ways, from profound insights about God and the future of Israel, to secret messages exclusively hidden and revealed only to the most holy among us, to the raving visions of a person suffering from schizophrenia—a mental disorder that distorts reality, often in the form of hallucinations.

The truth is that no one knows for certain, but I strongly agree with the "profound insights about God and the future of Israel and the temple" opinion for three reasons:

1. Ezekiel didn't have just one extraordinary vision, but six, and they were shared along with a series of prophecies and symbolic acts that taken together offer a consistent critique of current worship practices in Babylon and at the temple in Jerusalem, the need for individual accountability to God and repentance, the eventual restoration of Israel, and the rebuilding of the temple in Jerusalem. The visions are not

one-off pointless ravings, but part of a powerful message of responsibility, repentance, renewal, and hope.

2. When describing his visions, Ezekiel consistently used the word "like." For example, in his first vision (found in chapter 1), "like" appears twenty times: "like glowing metal" (v. 4), "like four living creatures" (v. 5), "like those of a calf" (v. 7), "like burnished bronze" (v. 7), "their faces looked like this" (v. 10), "like burning coals of fire" (v. 13), "like torches" (v. 13), "like flashes of lightening" (v. 14), "like topaz" (v. 16), "like a wheel" (v. 16), "like a vault" (v. 22), "sparkling like crystal" (v. 22), "like the roar of rushing waters" (v. 24), "like the voice of the Almighty" (v. 24), "like the tumult of an army" (v. 24), "like a throne" (v. 26), "like that of a man" (v. 26), "like glowing metal" (v. 27), "like fire" (v. 27), and "like the appearance of a rainbow" (v. 28). And the chapter ends with this explanation: "This was the appearance of the likeness of the glory of the Lord" (v. 1:28b). To me, this description identifies the use of comparisons and metaphors (like this and like that) in an attempt to describe something that is almost inexpressible rather than an argument for the reality of his visions.

3. Throughout the book, when God speaks to Ezekiel, he is called "Son of Man" (ninety-three times). Son of Man, Son of Adam, Son of Dust (depending on the translation), but not Son of God. There is no delusion here about who is God and who is not. God (Ezekiel reports) makes it abundantly clear—there is no imputed divinity for this vision keeper.

What can we say about seeing visions today? First, we are unlikely to experience Ezekiel's kind of a fantastic string of visions. It's certainly not crazy if we do, but experience tells me that most of us won't. However, I do believe that God gives many of us a vision from time to time—a vision for a new ministry in the community or church, a fresh start in a marriage, a better affordable-housing response, a deeper sense of community in our neighborhood, or an innovative way to minister to families in crisis. If one has the courage to share a vision of that sort, it shouldn't be simply dismissed, even if such an idea has been tried in the past. New visions deserve to be heard, must be heard, but there is no obligation to rush into a commitment to proceed without adequate planning, resources, and support. In fact, when we do, it lessens the likelihood of bringing even a very timely vision to fruition.

Second, we should be suspicious of visions that further a personal agenda or personal gain. While chairing the search committee for a new university president, I was approached by a man who told me that in the vision he saw his wife serving as the next president, giving her inaugural speech. He pressed me to call off the search and simply send his wife's name to the board of trustees for their affirmation. Needless to say, I declined, and I told him that I believed that God would want us to honor the process and see things out. I still do. Proposed shortcuts always make the priest in me a bit nervous. (By the way, his wife didn't get the job.)

Finally, visions come with a good deal more credibility when the "visioner" is willing to invest their own time, energy, resources, and identity to bring the vision to reality. It's a cautionary sign when those who have visions for the church or for us are unwilling to step up and step in themselves. I worked with a colleague who would come running across campus yelling my name, "Dean Allen, Dean Allen, do you know what you should do?" He always had a project in mind for me but was too busy to lend a hand. When I saw him coming, I would walk the other way before he saw me if I could.

In summary, we should thank God for new visions, especially about building the kingdom. We sorely need them, even if we can't pursue every vision. They need to be properly vetted. We must be cautious of visions that promote power, confusion, or personal agendas. God doesn't work that way. We do that all on our own.

And we must face the reality that even if we believe our vision is spot on and deeply needed, others may disagree. Change is very difficult, especially if others draw their energy and identity from the status quo. In such cases, the prophet is often shown the door, figuratively, and sometimes literally. Both are painful and leave their mark. Being a prophet is not for the faint of heart, and not the easiest way to win a popularity contest. That's why it is so important to speak at God's initiation, not our own.

Using Sign Acts

Throughout the Old Testament, prophets used a variety of means to get their messages across, including sign acts or demonstration prophecies. Ezekiel was no exception, constructing a model of Jerusalem under siege, laying on his side in silence with legs bound by ropes, cooking his meals over a cow dung fire, rationing his water, and pushing a bag with all his belongings through a hole he made in the city wall—all to demonstrate the future siege and impending fall of Jerusalem. He must have been the talk of the neighbors. Actions do speak louder than words. They always have.

So, what can we learn from the ancient use of sign acts as we go about our daily activities today? How can we share the light of Christ and the bright-winged presence of the Holy Spirit in our own community? Let me suggest three simple, modern-day sign acts that speak volumes to those we love and care about. One of the most powerful sign acts we can do is to prepare a meal for a neighbor, a friend, or even a stranger in need—and drop it off. Nothing needs to be said; you've said it all.

Another powerful sign act is simply to pay attention, to find out about the schedule of the children in your church or neighborhood and attend their recitals or ball games or choir performances. Be there and be proud of the kids. Your presence will be noted and appreciated by their parents. Again, nothing more needs to be said.

And a third sign act is to show up for the full range of church events, even if you'd rather be home taking a nap or watching a ball game. None of us can be excited or interested in every activity or service at our church, but others in the congregation have put a good deal of time and effort into the concert, a special sale, a public recital, an annual meeting, or an early Easter service. When you show up, smile, and lend support, you speak volumes without saying a word.

Sign acts help us practice the habit of holy silence. Of course, not all silence is holy, but providing a meal, being present in the lives of others, and simply showing up certainly can be. In so many instances, the practice of holy silence ministers to others, and we are shaped and formed in good ways as we practice.

Challenging Theology

Many Israelites believed that they were living in Babylonian exile because of the sins of their nation, not because they had personally sinned in any way. They believed that the sins of the nation were held against everyone, even if they were individually faithful and without guilt. They were in exile as a form of corporate punishment, so there was no need for repentance. In fact, there was nothing they could do about it. Ezekiel challenged their understanding of sin and accountability.

In addition, many exiles believed that since Yahweh resided in the temple in Jerusalem and was not personally with them in the same sense in Babylon, they were on their own, free to incorporate other local gods in their worship. It couldn't hurt anything, and it might help. Through his visions and prophecies, however, Ezekiel made it clear that Yahweh's presence was not limited to the temple. In fact, Yahweh was with them in Babylon too, in exile, and everyone was accountable for their individual actions. Many were not living faithfully, but with repentance there was the hope of restoration and renewal.

This theology of personal responsibility, repentance, forgiveness, and restoration was new to many exiles, and we don't know how Ezekiel's messages were received. What we do know is that a remnant did return from the Babylonian exile some years later, so his theological challenges couldn't have fallen completely on deaf ears. Beyond that, we just don't know.

So, what about us? Are we called to challenge another's theology, and if so, how do we go about this task? Let me share this caution at the outset—challenging someone's theology is risky business, to say the least, and more times than not the most appropriate thing to say is to say nothing at all. Like Ezekiel, we go back to our house and say nothing until and unless we know for certain that it is an issue that we are called to address. In most cases, we can just let it go, and let the Holy Spirit do the heavy lifting.

If we do feel the need to challenge a particularly harmful theological view, I believe it is best done while functioning as a priest, not a prophet. Prayerful discretion about what, when, and how to challenge a theological belief is crucial, and such discussions are always best done with humility, sensitivity, kindness, and in relationship.

Ultimately, I believe we are called to be lovers, not fighters, and trying to correct someone's theology in the name of good theology (usually our own) will lead to a fight or fracture more times than not. Better to practice holy silence and love our neighbor, offering friendship, understanding, and grace—the very way we would want to be treated by our neighbors, particularly if they don't agree with our theology. As it turns out, this street runs both ways.

Offering Hope

I've already mentioned how Ezekiel interwove words of hope along with his blistering critiques and foreboding prophecies. In my view, it was a supreme act of spiritual kindness. I think most of us are better at offering critiques and criticisms than at offering words of encouragement and hope. Like many of the prophets of old, we are better at blowing in, blowing off, and blowing out rather than at staying put and living in the midst of the community who must consider and respond to our words of judgment. Ezekiel stayed put. He was in exile too, and he and his wife lived in the neighborhood. I think residence changes everything.

One final word about hope, and it has to do with Ezekiel's famous vision about dry bones coming to life in a strange valley. He saw "a great many bones on the floor of the valley, and they were very dry" (Ezek 37:2a). As I read it, he saw a huge pile of bones in the middle of a desert valley, a desolate and totally hopeless situation, yet the Lord promised to breathe new life into them. What a promise! God promises to bring new life and hope in the most unlikely places, and I take it to mean in our lives too, especially when our spirits are dry, our faith is weak, and our hopes are gone. Dry bones will rise like an army with a new spirit—that's a promise. Thanks be to God!

CLOSING COMMENTS

The more I read and learned about the prophet Ezekiel the more it captured my imagination, and the more it challenged how I live my life today. My prayer is that in some small way it will do the same for you.

The book of Ezekiel can be read and celebrated as a fantastic example of telling the truth, staying engaged, and offering grace. Ezekiel was a truth teller to be sure, but he also knew when to keep quiet, to let his life speak, demonstrating the familiar adage that actions speak louder than words. His forty days were spent in silence in full view of his neighbors, his fellow exiles. He had a hard and unwelcome message to share in his own neighborhood. The Lord told him that it wouldn't be easy, and that proved to be true, but he faithfully did as he was told to do. Then, he headed home. Ezekiel's witness has challenged me to embrace the practice of holy silence more fully. I hope you will join me in this formative spiritual discipline. For the next forty days and nights, let's let our actions, indeed our lives, speak of God's grace and faithfulness to us, even as we demonstrate the same to our neighbors.

CHAPTER SIX
Reversals—Jonah

> *Jonah began by going a day's journey into the city, proclaiming, "Forty more days and Nineveh will be overthrown." The Ninevites believed God. . . . When God saw what they did and how they turned from their evil ways, he relented and did not bring on them the destruction he had threatened.*
>
> —JONAH 3:4-5A,10

INTRODUCTION

THE BOOK OF EZEKIEL and the book of Jonah couldn't be more different. Ezekiel is long and complex, forty-eight chapters reporting strange visions, harsh prophecies, interesting sign acts, stern warnings, and outright condemnations about idol worship and personal accountability, but also threaded with genuine words of hope to the exiles in Babylon about their eventual return and the restoration of the temple in Jerusalem. Jonah, on the other hand, is a story told in four short chapters about a prophet who flees God's calling, gets a second chance, begrudgingly does what he is told to do, and then becomes angry because God doesn't follow through with what Jonah prophesied would happen—and what he dearly wanted to happen! We are left at the end of the story wanting to know more about what happened next. We simply don't know.

The book of Jonah is the only prophetic book in the Bible that does not relay God's messages directly to the people of Israel: "This is what the Lord says . . ." Instead, it is a short and incomplete story about what happened to a prophet named Jonah who (finally) went to Nineveh. From this story, however, we can draw several important theological conclusions about the nature of God, about the power of repentance, and about the mystery of grace. So, at the end of the day, it is not a simple story about Jonah and the whale: it is a story about God. And as you will see, this simple story is rich, profound, and wise—not a simple story at all. There's a lot going on behind the curtain.

Jonah

Second Kings is the only other book in the Hebrew Bible to mention Jonah, a prophet living in the eighth century BCE who foretold the restoration and expansion of the Northern Kingdom during the reign of Jeroboam II: "He [King Jeroboam] was the one who restored the boundaries of Israel from Lebo Hamath to the Dead Sea, in accordance with the word of the Lord, the God of Israel, *spoken through his servant Jonah son of Amittai, the prophet from Gath Hepher*" (2 Kgs 14:25; italics mine). Geth Hepher was a border town in the Northern Kingdom of Israel. We hear nothing more about his activities in Israel until he appears as the central figure in the book of Jonah, one of the twelve books of the minor prophets in the Bible.

Interestingly, Jesus mentions Jonah and invites this association: "For as Jonah was three days and three nights in the belly of a huge fish, so the Son of Man will be three days and three nights in the heart of the earth" (Matt 14:40). As you might expect, Jesus' words as reported in both Matthew and Luke have given rise to a myriad of speculations, explanations, justifications, and arguments too. Later in the chapter, we'll revisit this important theological connection.

(A sidenote: each year, the entire book of Jonah is read in synagogues all over the world on Yom Kippur—the Day of Atonement—the holiest day of the year in Judaism. It is another example of the power and influence of this not-so-simple story.)

The Ninevites

The Ninevites were residents of Nineveh, the capital city of the Neo-Assyrian empire. The city was located on the east bank of the Tigris River at the intersection of several major trade routes, making it one of the most important and flourishing cities in its day. In fact, at one time, Nineveh was arguably the largest city in the entire world.

In Jonah's time, however, Assyrians were known for the ruthless conquest and domination of their neighbors in the region. In particular, the Assyrian army was greatly feared because of its brutality and torture of anyone who opposed their occupation and rule, and the government was known for its well-planned, systematic exile of conquered peoples, including, at one time, the Northern Kingdom of Israel. Assyrian exile brought emotional devastation to the conquered people, and economic devastation to the occupied regions. These factors, along with a manner of worship that violated many of the commandments known to the Israelites, made the Ninevites some of the most feared and despised people on the face of the earth. When told to go to Nineveh and preach against it, is it any wonder that Jonah's first response was to run the other way? What would you do?

Forty Days and Nights

Before we revisit the ancient story of Jonah and explore some takeaways for our lives today, I want to mention just a word or two about the forty days and nights found in this evergreen story. For the Ninevites, forty days and nights represented a time for repentance before the other shoe dropped, to try to make things right with the desperate hope of a reversal. They sincerely hoped that God might show mercy on them. For Jonah, forty days and nights represented a time of patiently waiting until the other shoe did drop—on Nineveh. They would finally get what they deserved, and he wanted to be on hand to witness it. Jonah could hardly wait.

The forty days also represented a time of reversal on God's part—showing great mercy to the Ninevites, and a time of reversal for Jonah too, leaving him disappointed, angry, and embarrassed. Perhaps we can recall a time or two when God did not do exactly what we told others that God should do and would do, but instead showed more grace and mercy than anyone deserved—especially to those we didn't like.

At the end of the day, these forty days and nights of transitions and reversals are about all of us too.

THE STORY OF JONAH

Even as a young child, I was captivated by the story of Jonah. While growing up in rural Michigan and fishing fresh water lakes most of the summer, my brothers and I had many discussions about just how big a fish would have to be to swallow a man, and what we would do if we ever hooked on to such a trophy. Obviously, there wouldn't be room in the boat, so we would lash the fish to the side of the boat, row back to shore with all our might, tie the boat to the dock, then run for help. Fortunately for us, we never had to put our plan, such as it was, into action. We became convinced that the great fish must be a saltwater variety, and since we were nearly a thousand miles from the Atlantic Ocean, it seemed quite unlikely that we would ever have the chance to land the beast. As it turns out, we were right.

We would often ask our grandmother to tell us her version of the story of Jonah during our bedtime prayers, and she would oblige us with a spirited rendition about running away from God and ending up in the fish's belly, complete with sound effects of the great storm, the crashing waves, the wailing sailors, and even the gurgling stomach of the fish. Her story usually ended just as Jonah made it back to shore—safe and sound (and smelly), but finally ready to do God's will.

In what follows, I'll try to fill in some important story details that my grandmother left out at bedtime and offer some insights from the story that are relevant to our lives today. I believe there are plenty.

Jonah Flees

When the word of the LORD came to Jonah—"Go to the great city of Nineveh and preach against it, because its wickedness has come up before me" (Jonah 1:2)—it must have come as a shock. For one thing, Jonah hadn't been all that active as a prophet, living in a small border town. It wasn't in the middle of nowhere, but you could see it from there. For another thing, it was surprising that God would just now notice Nineveh's wickedness. After all, they had been wicked for a very long time. They were a nasty people. When their captive enemies arrived at Nineveh, they never went home again. They simply disappeared. And to top it off, Jonah was to go and "preach against it" (Jonah 1:1). The text doesn't say what it meant to "preach against it" but Jonah had every right to wonder if he would simply disappear too.

So, Jonah ran away, fleeing in the opposite direction. Nineveh was off to the east, so he headed west to Joppa where he booked passage to Tarshish, somewhere in the western Mediterranean, maybe as far away as Spain. It was as far away from Nineveh as one could get in the known world. On the way, however, the ship encountered a violent storm, causing all aboard to stop and pray to their own gods—all, that is, except Jonah. He was belowdecks, sound asleep. We are not told why, but when you are running away from God, sleep is often the only distraction you have.

The sailors worked feverishly to save the ship, throwing cargo overboard to lighten the weight of the ship, all to no avail. After casting lots and confronting him, Jonah admitted that he was the reason for the storm. He told the sailors that they could save the ship by throwing him overboard. Even then, they tried gallantly to row back to land, but when it became apparent that they couldn't make it, they threw Jonah over the rails and into a very angry sea. But as they did, they asked God to forgive them—just in case he was innocent. They didn't need to worry.

"The raging sea grow calm. At this, the men greatly feared the Lord, and they offered a sacrifice to the Lord and made vows to him" (Jonah 1:15b–16). To be honest, we do not know how long the sailors' fear of the Lord lasted or how long they kept their vows, but it was certainly a good start.

And what about Jonah? This is the part of the story that we all know from Sunday School: "Now the Lord provided a huge fish to swallow Jonah, and Jonah was in the belly of the fish for three days and three nights" (Jonah 1:17). Over the centuries, countless hours have been spent trying to nuance the story or to prove or disprove the idea that one can live in a fish (or a sea monster) for three days. What I think is much more pertinent to the story of Jonah is that while he was in grave distress, fearing for his life at the bottom of the sea, he prayed: "But I, with shouts of grateful praise, will sacrifice to you. What I have vowed I will make good. I will say, 'Salvation comes from the Lord'" (Jonah 2:9).

And what was the response? "And the Lord commanded the fish, and it vomited Jonah onto dry land" (Jonah 2:10). Think of it. In the darkest moment of Jonah's life and in the most terrible and terrifying place he had ever been, all due to his own rebellion, God heard and responded to his prayers with mercy. I think there is a lesson here for all of us, if we have ears to hear.

As a result, he was sitting on dry ground, a bit disoriented and unsure what to do next. Was he finally ready to obey God's instructions to go to Nineveh and preach against them? Apparently, he was. Being delivered from a terrible place after three days has a way of clearing your head. Now the story gets interesting, full of unexpected twists and turns.

A Second Chance

It shouldn't come as a surprise that God gave Jonah a second chance. Every person we have read about thus far in this book received a second chance of one kind or another. Moses was commissioned to lead the Israelites out of Egypt even after he killed an Egyptian and fled for his life. David continued as king long after his confession of an affair with Bathsheba and arranging for her husband's life to be taken in battle. Elijah was given a new task even after organizing a self-serving show on Mount Carmel that ultimately led to the needless slaughter of the prophets of Baal. Ezekiel was called as a prophet five years after being taken from his priestly post in Jerusalem and sent into Babylonian captivity; and in a theological sense, Noah represented a second chance on behalf of all creation.

And we could add so many more stories about receiving a second chance. For example, Jacob, whose name could be translated "He cheats," a name he surely earned on more than one occasion, was given a new name and a promise of a new life. Joseph, who was sold into Egyptian slavery by his brothers, rose to power and ultimately offered a second chance to his brothers and his people. And perhaps the most memorable story of a second chance, Jesus forgave Peter for his threefold denial on the night of his arrest and offered him a second chance to build the church. He took the offer and ran!

And when we think about getting a second chance, might we add our own stories about how God has offered to each of us grace upon grace—and a second chance. We have all received at least one. So, when you think about it, it is not out of line to use the phrase "the God of the Second Chance" because that's who God is and that's what God does.

Back to Jonah's second chance. Scripture tells us, "Then the word of the Lord came to Jonah a second time. Go to the great city of Nineveh and proclaim to it the message I give you" (Jonah 3:1–2). Now, to be fair, we are not told exactly what message Jonah was given to proclaim to the Assyrians, but it seems likely that it was some type of warning that if they didn't repent, they would face destruction of one kind or another in forty days. If not, why would Jonah need to go at all if the consequences were predetermined? We don't know, but we do know that Jonah went for the short version: "Forty days more and Nineveh will be overthrown" (Jonah 3:4b). That was his entire message. It seems likely that Jonah wanted the Ninevites to get what they deserved. However, we are told that the Ninevites took the warning seriously, proclaimed a citywide fast, put on sackcloth (even on the animals), prayed for mercy, and promised to give up their evil ways. "When God saw what they did and how they turned from their evil ways, he relented and did not bring on them the destruction he had threatened" (Jonah 3:10).

Jonah's Anger

God showed mercy to the nastiest people on the face of the earth, and Jonah didn't like it a bit. After all, the Assyrians were a hated enemy and, more personally, his credibility was on the line. How was one to be a prophet of doom if God didn't back him up, willing to relent at the last moment? As Scripture tells us, "To Jonah this seemed very wrong, and he was angry" (Jonah 4:1). "I knew it! I just knew that you would do something like this," Jonah complained, "since you are gracious, compassionate, slow to anger, and abounding in love. I did what you told me to do, but you didn't back me up. Now I feel like a fool, and I might as well die!" I don't know if these are the exact words Jonah used, but I think the sentiment is spot on.

He went outside the city and made himself a shelter in the shade, still hoping that Nineveh would be torched in one way or another, but the only thing that went the way of all flesh was the leafy plant that had given him shade that day. Again, the story tells us that Jonah wanted to die. God challenged Jonah about his anger over the loss of a single leafy plant: "If you are so angry and concerned about one solitary plant, why shouldn't I, the LORD, be concerned about an entire city—including the animals?" (Jonah 4:10–11).

At that point, God didn't mention about how nasty the Ninevites were or how deserving they were of a swift and just punishment. I guess in God's economy that wasn't part of the calculation. And there is no mention of Jonah's response. In fact, there is no real ending to the story. What happened to the Ninevites? We do not know. How long were they faithful to their promises? Again, we don't know. What happened to Jonah? Did he go into the city and celebrate with the Assyrians? Highly unlikely. Did he go back home to his family? We don't know that either. What we do know with certainty is this: the love and grace of God is beyond our wildest imagination, showing up in the most unlikely places and most unlikely times in our lives, and for that we, all of us, should be eternally grateful.

DISCUSSION

I think my mother saved my soul. I really do. Of course, I know that Jesus played the leading role, but honestly, my mother was a close second. She taught me at a young age that I didn't have to have everything figured out to be a true believer. In fact, in many ways, my faith was made stronger by asking hard questions and struggling with honest doubts rather than by memorizing the few correct answers accompanied by a proof text suitable for embroidery on a sofa pillow. She was adamant that a faith demanding certainty without room for doubts wasn't deep enough to get me past the ninth grade. In her house, questions would always be welcome.

So it was when I asked her about Jonah being swallowed by a great fish. How could this be? It just didn't make a lot of sense to me. "Well," she would say, "let's talk about this together." And we did. In this last section, I want to revisit my question about the reality of a huge fish and highlight several key theological insights that we can appropriate from the story of Jonah, a book deserving to be read in its entirety every year by every church I know.

What About That Huge Fish?

Honestly, I don't think it matters, at least not for the intended message and moral of Jonah's story. I was taught by a very wise teacher that the assumptions you bring to any text will largely determine how you read the text and filter what truths you take from it. I think this is true when reading any Old Testament story, and particularly applicable when reading Jonah. Is this story meant to be taken historically, as a literal report of an actual event, and must we do so as a demonstration of faith, or could the story of Jonah be a form of fiction, told to convey some insights about God and what God expects of all of us, a story that forms and informs our faith?

I think we all know what it means to take a story literally, to believe that every aspect of the story actually happened in human time. This is the dominant approach to reading Scripture in many conservative protestant communities, and efforts to find scientific evidence that someone could survive three days in the belly of a great fish continue to this very day. Beyond the efforts to find a scientific explanation, there is also a line of belief that this event was a miracle that shows that God does act from time to time beyond our human understanding of reality. It is simply another illustration of God's power along with calming storms, healing lepers, giving sight to the blind, feeding thousands with a few loaves of bread, or raising Lazarus from the dead. We accept them as an act of faith.

But what if the story of Jonah was a form of fiction? Does that denigrate the value and sacredness of it? Does it make Jonah any less profound or true? For many, the word "fiction" is a red flag, meaning that the story is unreliable, untrue, made up, and off limits as a matter of faith. However, I understand fiction differently. Of course, there are many kinds of fiction, but let me quickly list three forms of storytelling that could apply to Jonah: mythology, allegory, and parable.

A myth is a story of legendary proportion, often told in historical fashion, and usually involving a hero (or antihero). Myths often deal with deities in one form or another and are told to explain an event that is beyond the reality of our daily lives, or to undergird a particular practice or worldview. A myth is not a newspaper report of an actual event but rather a social teaching tool. Taken in this way, some scholars over the centuries have labeled the story of Jonah as a sacred myth teaching us that God is interested in everyone—even Ninevites.

A second form of storytelling is an allegory where, through symbolic, fictional characters, we are told a story that attempts to explain the nature of human existence or the meaning of life. In an allegory, the actors and events are related and represent something beyond the actual story. For example, understood as an allegory, Jonah might represent Israel, and his refusal to preach to Nineveh an indictment of Israel for their lack of concern for their neighbors. The terrible storm might represent the futility of running away from an angry God, and the great fish as a means of grace and a second chance for all of us. Of course, whether we see an angry or a loving God in the story depends a good deal on the concept of God we bring to the story.

A third form of storytelling is the parable, a form of teaching that Jesus used throughout his ministry. A parable is a short, fictional story told to make a particular moral or religious point. For example, Jesus told the parable of the good Samaritan to answer the question, Who is my neighbor? It is interesting to note that Jesus did not call these stories parables. He just told stories; the label was added later. To my knowledge, no one today is searching in Israel to find the remains of the landowner's vineyard (Matt 21:33–41) or the inn mentioned in the parable of the good Samaritan (Luke 10:25–37). Why? Because parables were always understood as theological, not historical.

At the end of the day, different ways of understanding Jonah come together when read first as theology, not as history. Ultimately, it is not a story about Jonah and the whale. Rather, it is a story about our God who never gives up on us—all of us. Thanks be to God.

Is There Really a Second Chance with God?

One of my best friends growing up believed that God had a perfect plan for his life, and his job was to stay the course and stay on the path. If he did, all would work out wonderfully. If, however, he lost his way and left the path for even a short step or two, God's perfect plan would be gone and could not be recovered; but if he earnestly repented, he might be offered a second-level, not-quite-so-good plan. God would still love and direct him, but on an alternate, minor-league, spiritual journey. And if he left this second-level, not-quite-so-good path, he would be toast. That would be the end of his life with God as he knew it. He would be doomed to hell. Honestly, he lived in constant fear that he would somehow unknowingly misstep and lose his way with God. In his theology, there was a chance for a not-quite-so-good second chance (of sorts), but clearly no third.

As I have already written in this chapter, I deeply believe that Scripture teaches us that we have a different kind of relationship with God, with the God of the Second Chance, a relationship that offers grace upon grace to all of us. In the Bible, there is story after story of a patient God offering grace and hope, chance after chance, to those who come up short—people just like us.

If the story of Jonah teaches us anything, it is that God is gracious and compassionate, slow to anger, abounding in love, and willing to relent from sending calamity (Jonah 4:2–3)—to Jonah, to the sailors, to the animals, and even to the Ninevites, the nastiest people on the face of the earth. If God extended grace in such a loving fashion to people like this, why would we believe that God would punish us for even the smallest misstep and send us on a last-chance, second-rate journey or straight to hell? That is not the heart of the loving God that I have come to know, and certainly not the heart of God as revealed in the story of Jonah.

Does God Care About the People We Don't Like?

Yes.

Hero or Antihero?

Jonah is an interesting figure. In some ways, Jonah is the hero of the story. He confessed to the sailors that he was the cause of their troubles and told them to throw him overboard, an act that would end his life but save theirs. This is a heroic act. And even though he didn't want to go to Nineveh, to the city of his hated enemy, he did, with remarkable success. This is the act of a hero too.

However, Jonah did run away from God, going in the opposite direction about as far away as he could get. That is not the act of a hero. And when he went to Nineveh, he prophesied the destruction of the Ninevites in forty days, but there is no record that he offered them any hope or recourse for their evil ways. It seems that he was eager to see them burn, to get what they deserved. Not so heroic. And when God did listen to the Ninevites and relent, Jonah was angry—and embarrassed too. This was quite human, but not the act of a hero.

In the last analysis, Jonah was both a hero and an antihero, so human. Maybe that's why it is easy to identify with the story of Jonah. It is a story about all of us too.

Why Is There No Ending to the Story?

Honestly, I don't know. It is certainly a curious way to end a very short but complex story that is ultimately about God, Jonah, and all of us too. It might be that to provide a storybook ending about Jonah and the Ninevites living happily ever after would be trite and unfaithful to the profound significance and purpose of the story, or it might be that the end of the story was lost or somehow forgotten. What if Jonah joined the Assyrians or just went on home or just died outside the city? Would any one ending be acceptable? Again, we do not know.

What we do know is because the story of Jonah ends so abruptly without a conclusion or resolution, it falls on each individual reader to connect the dots, to ponder what might have happened next. It pulls us in and draws us out. When you think about it, that's a brilliant ending.

CLOSING COMMENTS

The story of Jonah is a story of grace—to the Ninevites, to the sailors, to Jonah, and even to the animals (a rather curious aspect of the story). But where do we find ourselves in this story? Do we identify with the sailors who faced harm and distress because of the actions of others? Do we identify with the Ninevites who repented and received more grace than they could even imagine or deserve? Or do we identify with one of the many faces of Jonah: running away from doing what we know we should do, like extending an apology or offering forgiveness to a colleague or family member; crying out to God in the darkest place we have ever been and receiving a second chance; going through the motions and saying all the right things but privately hoping that others get what we think they deserve; or just sitting on the periphery as a spectator, unwilling to lift a finger to help and interested more in our own image? If the truth were to be told, most of us have played one of these roles, maybe more than one, at some time or another. In one sense, the story of Jonah is a deeply human story about all of us.

Fortunately, it is not just a story about all of us, able actors though we are. It is a story of God's relentless grace pursuing us, calling us, and hearing us, even when we disobey, even when we flee in the wrong direction and end up in the darkest place we could ever imagine at the bottom of the ocean. It is a story of God's great love, answering our prayers and offering us, all of us, hope, healing, and a second chance—or a third—or more. Thanks be to God!

CHAPTER SEVEN

Temptations—Jesus

Temptations don't always come the first day in the wilderness.
—*PATRICK ALLEN*

INTRODUCTION

MY WIFE IS A seminary graduate, and I confess that I sometimes sneak into her home office and borrow a few books from her library to gain a better understanding about whatever topic I am thinking or writing about at the time. As a result of my latest raid, I have a tall stack of New Testament books on my desk to help me understand a bit more about the nature and context of the temptation narratives found in all three Synoptic Gospels—Matthew, Mark, and Luke. I am truly humbled by the depth and precision of the scholarship I find, and I am thankful for those willing to give so much of their time and talents, indeed their lives, to the serious study of the Gospels. And I always come away reminded that serious scholars can disagree about a lot of things—and they do! That's one of the outcomes of vibrant and passionate scholarship that I admire, but I confess that at times it can be confusing to the locals in the pew, including me.

With that said, I have no intention of revisiting the numerous scholarly approaches and disagreements about how to understand the temptations of Jesus in the wilderness immediately after his baptism. That conversation has been going on for centuries, and it will continue. Rather, I want to look at the temptation narratives in the order in which they were written—Mark, Matthew, then Luke (most serious scholars agree on this progression) and see what we can glean from them about how to understand and deal with the temptations and trials we face when we find ourselves in the wildernesses, often one of our own making. And I'll close the chapter by offering a few thoughts about how to recognize some modern-day temptations that are incessantly advertised and encouraged in more ways than we can even imagine, and what it means to avoid their corrosive influence and remain faithful as we make our way home.

THE BAPTISM AND TESTING OF JESUS: MARK 1:9–12

The Baptism of Jesus

I love the book of Mark. When I read it, it feels like the author is rushing to get to the end of the story or working furiously to meet a publishing deadline. Impatient words, such as "immediately," "as soon as," "at once," and "then," keep the narrative moving, and about half the book is devoted to Jesus' travel to Jerusalem and his last days there. Mark tells us nothing about Jesus' birth, the journey to Egypt with his parents, his family, his boyhood, or times spent in the temple. The narrative starts with John the Baptist preaching in the wilderness and baptizing in the Jordan River, and it is there that Jesus joins him and is baptized.

As Mark tells it, "Just as Jesus was coming up out of the water, he saw heaven torn open and the Spirit descending on him like a dove. And a voice came from heaven: 'You are my Son, whom I love; and with you I am well pleased'" (1:10–11). At the very moment of his baptism, just as he is coming up out of the water, Jesus has a vision and receives the best affirmation one could ever hope for from a father: You are my son, part of the family. I love you, and with you I am well pleased. Knowledgeable readers at the time would certainly have recognized the echoes of Isa 42:1 and Ps 2:7 in these words, and one would think that anyone receiving such an enormous validation from heaven would be ready to immediately begin their public ministry, perhaps right there on the spot, but that isn't what happened: "At once the Spirit sent him out into the wilderness" (Mark 1:12).

Into the Wilderness

Into the wilderness, and not for a four-hour sightseeing trip in an ATV with a safari guide! No, it was forty days and forty nights, and he wasn't alone. Satan was there tempting him, but Mark doesn't go into much detail. We don't know how he was tempted, when he was tempted, how many times he was tempted, or how long each temptation lasted, but there is every reason to believe that Jesus came through with flying colors. And Mark also reports that Jesus was with the wild animals and attended by angels. The mention of wild animals is curious. Perhaps it was pointing back to the prophecies of Isaiah (11:6–9; 65:25) and Hosea (2:18) about a time when there would be peace, even peace with wild animals. We don't really know, but it sounds plausible.

What we do know is that Jesus' wilderness experience was sandwiched between the spiritual high point of his baptism and the start of his public ministry. Certainly, Jesus was tested in many ways throughout his ministry, but a huge test of his faithfulness came early on. I think there is a lesson here for all of us. The decisions we make and the actions we take when we are faced with temptations have their own moral trajectory; their arc takes us somewhere. They always do, and sometimes such temptations come when we are enjoying a high spiritual moment. It seems that we can be vulnerable to temptation in those moments as well as in our darkest moments, maybe even more so. It is comforting to remember that Mark tells us that Jesus was never alone, "Angels attended him" (Mark 1:13b), perhaps as they attended to Elijah in his wilderness experience (1 Kgs 19:5–8). I truly believe that angels will attend to us in the wildernesses we face too. It is grace upon grace.

JESUS IS TESTED IN THE WILDERNESS: MATT 3:16–4:11

The Baptism of Jesus

The writer of Matthew reports the baptism of Jesus by his cousin John in much the same fashion as does Mark. However, immediately after coming up out of the water, Matthew adds that what Jesus saw descending like a dove and alighting on him was the Spirit of God (3:16). Mark just mentions the Spirit coming down but given the fact that a dove is seen and a voice is heard coming from heaven, I'm sure most readers would have made the connection.

An additional piece of information reported in Matthew is that John was reluctant to baptize Jesus, arguing that Jesus should be doing the baptizing, deferring to Jesus' divine calling. However, Jesus convinces John otherwise, stating that being baptized by him would "be proper in this way for us to fulfill all righteousness" (3:15). I love the "us" in this passage. Jesus couldn't do his work alone—neither can we.

Tested in the Wilderness

In various English translations of the Bible, the words "tempted" and "tested" are used interchangeably in this passage. Of course, any temptation is a test of one kind or another, but not all tests are necessarily a temptation. There are other kinds of tests, and some of the tests we face can actually be good for us. As my father loved to say, "They build character." Later in this chapter, we will look at some contemporary tests and how we are shaped by our responses to them, but for now, we'll focus on the three temptations that Jesus faced in the wilderness. There is much to be learned as we negotiate our own forty days and nights in the wildernesses of life.

After Forty Days and Nights

Temptations don't always come the first day in the wilderness. Honestly, I wish they did. We could anticipate their coming a bit easier and we would be in better condition to deal with them, but that's not how it goes. As Matthew tells us, "Then Jesus was led by the Spirit into the wilderness to be tempted by the devil. After fasting forty days and nights, he was hungry. The tempter came to him" (4:1–3a). The tempter comes after forty days and forty nights. Notice the mention of forty nights too. When you're isolated, tired, and hungry, the nights can be particularly long and painful, and your mind is vulnerable to a wide range of negative thoughts, suggestions, and decisions. I'm sure the tempter understood that.

Stones into Bread

After forty days and nights, Jesus was hungry. Who wouldn't be? Hunger in one form or another reduces our ability to think straight and make good decisions. It attacks mind, body, and spirit. Simply put, hunger can be nasty. Is it any wonder that the devil's first temptation was to tell Jesus to turn stones into bread? Surely he had the power to do so, and what could possibly be wrong with taking care of your own physical needs? If you were terribly hungry and had the power to turn stones into bread, what would you do?

Of course, it wasn't that simple. Temptations never are, no matter how they present themselves or how good we are a rationalizing our own actions. In this case, the stones-to-bread suggestion was a bit of a ruse. It wasn't really about satisfying his hunger, but about being tempted, taunted really, into proving that he was the Son of God. After receiving an enormous affirmation from heaven at his baptism, his identity was well established. He knew who he was—he was God's Son, the Beloved, and his Father was well pleased with him. He didn't need to prove anything to the devil, or to anyone else for that matter.

It is interesting that the tempter started with bread. I'm sure Jesus was mindful of Israel's desire for bread in the wilderness, and how God first tested them and then provided manna when they were hungry (Deut 8:3), even though they came up short time after time—and I'm sure he was mindful that God would provide for him too. Jesus would remain faithful to his baptismal blessing. He answered, quoting from that same passage in Deuteronomy: "Man does not live by bread alone, but on every word that comes from the mouth of God" (Matt 4:4). I'm sure that God was well pleased with his answer too.

Throw Yourself Down

Not nearly ready to concede the day, the devil next takes Jesus by way of a vision to the Holy City, positions him on the highest point of the temple, and offers this familiar frame: "If you are the Son of God" (Matt 4:5). Same hook, but this time a different bait. The devil, quoting from Ps 91 as a proof text, tries to convince Jesus to jump off the temple and have the angels rush in and carry him to a safe (and very public) landing. I'm sure the devil made a good case: "Think about it. Isn't this a good way to start your public ministry, Jesus? In a culture that is obsessively interested in seeing spectacular signs and wonders, this will be the ultimate showstopper! It will validate your identity and propel your public ministry. Even though you're from the sticks, you will instantly become a major player in Jerusalem's religious scene; no, *the* major player, someone who commands an audience in the highest of places. And think of all the good you can do! What could possibly be wrong with promoting yourself just a little bit—for the sake of your ministry?"

Of course, Matthew doesn't give us much detail at this point, and I don't know how the devil made his case, but it could have been along those lines. At the very least, I have to admit that this is the kind of argument that would have persuaded me to take a leap from just about anywhere—all for the sake of the kingdom, of course. If I'm honest, I have to admit that when it comes to being tested in the wilderness, I'm more like the Israelites than I would like to admit. How about you?

Regardless of the strength of the devil's temptation, Jesus isn't interested in becoming an instant success. Instead, he quotes from Deuteronomy: "Do not put the Lord your God to the test" (6:16). Apparently, the "If you are the Son of God" ruse wasn't going to work, so in a third temptation, the devil raises the stakes in more ways than one.

On a Very High Mountain

We move from isolation and hunger in the wilderness (first temptation), to the temple in the very heart of Jerusalem (second temptation), and now to the top of the world, a place where "all the kingdoms of the world and their splendor" could be seen (Matt 4:8). Of course, this was more than just an interesting geography lesson. Jesus isn't being shown all the kingdoms of the world to improve his map reading ability; he is shown all their splendor too. For me, that is the key. Having land and authority is nice, but having splendor takes ownership to an entirely new dimension. All Jesus had to do, he was told, was to bow down and worship the devil. If he did, he would be given all the splendor he could imagine, even more.

Jesus passes this test too, and on one level it seems like the easiest test of the three to pass. Was he really going to bow down and worship the devil in order to be given all the world, not knowing if the devil actually had control of all that was promised in return or if the devil would actually give away all the splendor to Jesus even if it was his to give? So, on this level, it seems like a fairly weak temptation. No thanks!

However, I don't want to underestimate the power of the promise of riches, particularly riches beyond imagination. After all, Jesus was a carpenter's son from Bethlehem, not the center of power or prosperity for anyone. Over my career, I've seen more than one good person lose their way, tempted by a few pieces of silver or a brief time in the spotlight on the platform. So the promise of all the kingdoms and their splendor was a really big deal, but Jesus didn't budge. Instead, he quotes from Deuteronomy one more time and tells the tempter to get lost.

Apparently, the devil got the message and left the scene. However, there is nothing in the text to suggest that this was a winner-take-all victory or that conflict with the devil was now over. No such luck. As it turns out, Jesus was tested throughout his ministry—a lesson for all of us too.

THE BAPTISM AND TEMPTATIONS ACCORDING TO LUKE: 3:21–23; 4:1–13

The temptation narratives in Matthew and Luke follow essentially the same outline: Jesus' baptism, led into the wilderness for forty days and nights, and the devil coming with three temptations, but there are some interesting additions in Luke's version. For example, Luke shows Jesus to be praying when the Holy Spirit descends upon him after his baptism (3:21). Matthew makes no mention of this. And Luke, after reporting that Jesus was thirty years old when he began his ministry, follows with Jesus' genealogy, demonstrating among other things that Jesus was in the messianic line of King David. Interestingly, the writer of Matthew also shares a genealogy of Jesus early on in the first Gospel, but there are differences. Matthew traces the lineage through David's son Solomon while Luke traces the lineage through another of David's sons, Nathan. The reasons for these two different lineages have been debated for centuries. Although this entire scholarly discourse is well beyond the scope of this book, I do recommend that you learn more about it if you are so inclined.

Luke also tells us that Jesus was tempted for the entire forty days, not just after forty days, and "when the devil had finished all this tempting, he left [Jesus] until an opportune time" (4:13). "An opportune time" doesn't sound like the devil was through testing Jesus. In fact, he wasn't. Sadly, temptation can be an ongoing ordeal for all of us.

Perhaps the most interesting difference between the temptation accounts in Matthew and Luke is the order of the temptations.

Matthew's account lists (1) turn stones into bread, (2) on the highest point of the temple, and then (3) on a high mountain. Luke's order reverses temptations two and three. Of course, no one really knows why, but it might be that Luke places the last temptation at the temple in Jerusalem, the place central to the Jewish faith, and to the life, death, and resurrection of Jesus. Again, we can't be certain. For me, such differences are interesting, something to ponder, something to study, a mystery of sorts, but certainly not a threat to my faith. I trust it is the same for you.

WHAT ABOUT US?

When I teach a small group Bible study, I find it is often helpful to try to locate ourselves in the story. For example, in the story of the prodigal son, do we most identify with the impatience and foolishness of the younger son, with the anger and condemnation of the older son, or with the grace and joy of the father? If you're like me, at one time or another, you've been all three.

So, what about the temptations we face, particularly in the wilderness? Which of the three would be most likely to test you: to take matters into your own hands, do it your own way, and let others see a master at work; to be widely recognized as gifted, committed, talented, and deeply spiritual; or to have influence, social standing, and stuff—lots of stuff. At times they can be a nasty hook for all of us.

In our culture, the driving values are appearance, achievement, and affluence, and they are promoted relentlessly on every media platform I know. We are told: *if* your hair or skin or clothes look like this, you drive that luxury car, you have the corner office or don't need to work at all, you have the house of our dreams, *then* you are really somebody important, someone special, and life is perfect—like the pictures posted from Disneyland. These are the twenty-first century temptations in a first-world country, and they are alive and well in our churches too.

Of course, deep down we know life doesn't work like that, that there are other values far more important, more centered, more kingdom oriented than appearance, achievement, and affluence, but they are *so* seductive, aren't they? What if we worked consciously and persistently every day to see the kingdom come in our everyday lives, to practice and celebrate values that not only shape us but also define us? What if we put character, calling, and compassion first? What if these were the values worth working for, worth fighting for, worth living for? If we did, I think the tempter would leave us too, and wait for an opportune time to return, but with the bright-winged presence of the Holy Spirit in our lives, maybe, just maybe, there wouldn't be another opportune time. I think when Jesus said, "Worship the Lord your God and serve him only" (Luke 4:8), he was saying much the same thing.

CLOSING COMMENTS

When the devil tempted Jesus, he quoted Scripture like a scholar. Indeed, he was. It is just a caution that not everyone who comes citing Scripture has your best interests or the best interests of the kingdom in mind.

CHAPTER EIGHT

Disbelief—Jesus and His Followers

Then the eleven disciples went to Galilee, to the mountain where Jesus had told them to go. When they saw him, they worshiped him; but some doubted.

—MATT 28:16-17

INTRODUCTION

The First Year on the Job

"They worshiped him, but some doubted," Matthew tells us (28:17). I can certainly relate to that, at least to the doubting part. In my work as a university provost/academic dean, I'm sure I wasn't the object of anyone's worship (faculties just don't do that sort of thing, and shouldn't), but I had my share of doubters, and they were happy to publicly share their concerns. In a faculty meeting in my very first semester as provost, a faculty member stood to his feet to give a committee report, and when he was finished, he added a few impromptu comments: "Our new dean isn't from around here. He didn't attend this university, and he is not from our denomination. He's not one of us. We don't really know him. He may have some plans for us, but I don't know if we can trust him. As far as I am concerned, the jury is still out on him and his ability to lead us."

As you might expect, I was stunned. Honestly, I had never been attacked like that before, and in such a public manner. Everyone looked at me for a response. I struggled to my feet and stumbled into speech: "Wow. I didn't see that coming. That really stings. While it is true that I am not from here, I am from somewhere, and that somewhere has shaped and formed me and prepared me for this challenge in good ways. I guess I thought that all this would have been considered during the interview process. In fact, I'm sure it was since I was asked about my background and preparation on more occasions than I can remember. Beyond this, I must say that I didn't know that the jury was still out on me. In fact, I didn't know that I was on trial! I came here to work with you to develop the most formative educational experience possible, to challenge students to live out their faith and worship God with everything they have and are—especially with their minds. I want to be a part of an educational community that works together to teach, shape, and send—to focus on instruction, formation, and vocation, because that's what I believe the best Christian universities do. I intend to show up every day to make that happen here. I want to work with you, not against you, and not in spite of you. We have an enormous opportunity in front of us. Let's not squander it by playing court. I'll just go ahead and plead guilty to whatever I am charged with and you can decide the sentence, but I'll be in my office tomorrow morning at 7:30 to go to work. I hope you'll join me in the challenge that is ours."

My comments were met with silence and blank stares—a smile or two would have been nice, but I didn't know how to read the room. I went home feeling like a stranger in a strange land. Maybe I wasn't welcome. Maybe this job wouldn't work out. Maybe it was too big for me. Their disbelief stung like a wasp, and I hardly slept. However, when I arrived at my office the next morning at 7:30, I was greeted by a group of my faculty colleagues—about fifty in total. They wanted me to know that as far as they were concerned, the trial was over and they were with me. Of course, I was deeply moved and told them so. "Let's go to work!" I said with a smile. We all did, but later in the day, a senior faculty member stopped by my office to let me know that there were still some doubters on the faculty, not a majority but a significant minority. I told her that they were my people too, and I would work for them as best I could, and I did, but it was a struggle at times. The stings kept coming.

It seems that there will always be doubters, no matter how hard you work or how well things are going. Some just can't see the progress or refuse to acknowledge that you are on the right track or the right person for the job. Maybe they wanted the job or thought that someone else would be better. I don't know, but I have replayed over and over again the start of my work at that university and what I might have said or done differently to win them over. To this day, I don't think there was anything else I could have said or done because deep down they didn't want to be won over. I wonder if Jesus ever had any similar thoughts. But some doubted, indeed.

Sharing My Doubts

I must confess that at times I have been the doubter too. Several years after the "doubting faculty meeting" incident, I was sitting in the president's leadership team meeting when the regional vice president of our food services company reported that our dearly loved and highly professional campus director of food services would be leaving for another assignment. He was recommending that the assistant director be promoted. During the discussion, I shared that I wasn't eager to see that promotion. In fact, I had some doubts about his ability to do the job. When pressed, I shared that I doubted that he had the interpersonal skills or an eye for detail that the director would need to be successful. I wondered if the assistant was ready, but that was just my opinion.

I thought that the regional vice president would go ahead and promote the assistant director, but that isn't what happened. The next day the assistant food services director came to my office and asked if he could have a word with me. We sat down in the ugly tan leather chairs that I inherited from the former dean. (I couldn't really get rid of them since he was now the president.) With tears in his eyes the assistant director told me that the regional vice president recounted in detail all the doubts that I shared in yesterday's meeting, and that he wouldn't be offered the job unless I gave my personal ok, a job he had been dreaming about for some time. All he wanted was a chance to prove himself. Now the tears were welling up in my eyes.

Honestly, I didn't know that my doubts would be taken that seriously or that they would sting so much. After a brief silence, I said, "I'm sorry that the doubts I shared hurt you and jeopardized your chances for a promotion. That wasn't my intent. I tried to share what I truly believed, but you deserve every chance to succeed. I just hope you know what big shoes you will be filling." He said he did. I called the VP and encouraged him to go ahead with the promotion. He did.

As it turns out, I had nothing to worry about. The assistant director quickly grew into the job and everyone agreed that he was one of the best directors ever. So much for my doubts. When I left the university several years later, I stopped by the food service director's office to say goodbye. I told him that I was wrong about him from the get-go, that my doubts were ill informed and unfair, and I was so proud of him for the work he was doing at the university. I also told him that if he ever needed a job recommendation, he could let me know and I would write a good one. Do you know what? He did—and I did. I told the prospective employer that he was the real deal—without a doubt. If they could hire him, they should in a New York minute. And they did!

How Could You Doubt Me After All This Time

I had been at the university for nearly a decade, and it was as close to a Camelot experience as I had ever known. Faculty morale was at an all-time high, and things were running smoothly. One day, however, two senior faculty members came to my office to register a serious complaint. One of their colleagues recently approached them and shared that the provost (me) was treating him unkindly, immorally, and illegally, and I was trying to run him off (his words). They told me that after praying about the situation, they felt they needed to report my misbehavior to both the faculty council and the president, but they wanted to talk to me first. I was shocked and wanted to give them an earful, but instead told them that while it was true that I had been dealing with their colleague, I couldn't go into detail with them without their colleague's permission. It was a matter of privacy, something that I had to honor even if their colleague did not. I assured them that they did not have all the facts and suggested that the four of us meet (if their colleague was agreeable). He was, so we met the next afternoon in the conference room next to my office.

After some small talk I suggested that I just share his personnel file, providing an overview of the events and actions of the past year. They all nodded, so I started reading. The file was nearly eight inches thick, but after sharing four or five reports I was told that I didn't need to go any further. They got the point; they were not told the truth about what was going on, and there was much more going on than they ever imagined. They apologized and got up to leave. I excused their colleague but asked the two senior colleagues to stay for a minute. They just stood there, looking at their feet.

"What is most hurtful," I said, "is that you doubted me. How could you believe what was said about me after all the years we have spent working together? Don't you know me by now? Why didn't you believe in me? I would never treat a colleague that way, but after a little prayer you were prepared to publicly attack me, to hurt me. I don't get it, not after all these years."

They apologized and hurried out. I do think they were sorry for their actions, or at least sorry that their conclusions were proven to be incorrect in an embarrassing way, but the sting remained. Why did they doubt me? Although on a totally different scale, a cosmic scale, I couldn't help thinking about how Jesus must have felt when some of his closest followers doubted him during the forty days and nights between his resurrection and his ascension.

"Then the eleven disciples went to Galilee, to the mountain where Jesus had told them to go. When they saw him, they worshiped him; but some doubted" (Matt 28:16–17). *Some doubted.* Wow!

DOUBTS AND DISBELIEF

I want us to look at how Jesus dealt with disbelief throughout his ministry, and particularly in the forty days and nights after his resurrection when he encountered disbelief among some of his most trusted disciples, those closest to him. I hope we can gain some insight that will help us when we face our own forty days and nights of disbelief, particularly from or with those closest to us.

Disbelief: Not the First Time

It seems that God in the Old Testament and Jesus in the New Testament were constantly faced with disbelief—in their words, in their warnings, in their signs, even in who they said they were. After a series of frustrations with the Israelites in the wilderness, God finally cried out to Moses, "How long will these people treat me with contempt? How long will they refuse to believe in me, in spite of all the signs I have performed among them?" (Num 14:11). Moses had to intercede to prevent the Lord from ending the exodus from Egypt right there on the spot. And that wasn't the only time that Moses found himself lying flat on the ground beseeching God on behalf of his people. How long indeed!

In his public ministry, Jesus faced his share of disbelief too. Matthew tells that while in prison, John the Baptist sent two of his disciples to ask Jesus, "Are you the one who is to come, or should we look for another?" (Matt 11:2–3), and they did so as Jesus was standing in a crowd. That had to sting. After all, they went way back. John must have heard stories about Mary's visit to his mother while they were both expecting, and it was John who baptized Jesus in the Jordan River. Did he forget that wonderful affirmation from God? Jesus had every right to be angry, and maybe he was tempted to send back a nasty message, but he didn't. He sent the messengers back with a report on what he had been doing and then turned to the crowd and told them that, as far as he was concerned, "among those born of women there has not risen anyone greater than John the Baptist . . . he is the Elijah who was to come" (Matt 11:14). He didn't belittle John. He didn't dismiss John. He praised him!

On another occasion, Jesus addressed the crowd that had followed him across the lake to the synagogue in Capernaum. When they asked for a sign that would help them believe in the one that God had sent to them, Jesus started into a very long and complicated discourse, including the assertion that it was necessary to drink his blood and eat his flesh to have eternal life. The crowd didn't understand what he was saying, nor did his own disciples. They wondered who could possibly accept such a hard teaching, and "many of his disciples turned back and no longer followed him" (John 6:66).

I think it was a make-or-break moment for his ministry, and Jesus must have sensed it. He turned to the Twelve and asked, "You do not want to leave too, do you?" (John 6:67). Peter jumped up and jumped in as he was always inclined to do, blurting out, "Lord, to whom shall we go? You have the words of eternal life. We have come to believe and know that you are the Holy One of God" (John 6:68). Satisfied with that affirmation of faith, Jesus and the Twelve set off, eventually heading for the Festival of Tabernacles in Jerusalem. There the disciples' faith would be put to the test, and it wouldn't be the last time.

Perhaps the most tender and honest confession about the lack of faith came from a father who wanted Jesus to heal his son who was possessed by an impure spirit. When Jesus told him that belief makes everything possible, the father responded: "I do believe; help my unbelief!" (Mark 9:24). In many ways, the father speaks for all of us. We do believe but help our unbelief. And what did Jesus do? He healed the boy right then and there!

FORTY DAYS AND NIGHTS—AFTER THE RESURRECTION

Ok, it might be one thing to not fully understand or believe Jesus' words about his future resurrection, but what about after the three days? What about the empty tomb? Mark tells us that when three women went to the tomb, they were told by a young man in a white robe that Jesus was not there—he had risen! They were then instructed to give the disciples a message. Instead, "trembling and bewildered, the women went out and fled the tomb. They said nothing to anyone because they were afraid" (Mark 16:8). And, I would add, because they were unprepared to believe what they saw and heard.

Luke picks up the story of the three women. Apparently, they did finally work up the courage to tell the disciples about their encounter at the tomb with the young man dressed in white. And what was their response? "They did not believe the women because their words seemed to them like nonsense" (Luke 24:11). Only Peter had the good sense to at least go and check it out. When he looked into the tomb, the only thing he saw were some strips of linen. "He went away, wondering to himself what had happened" (Luke 24:12b).

After Peter returned to the disciples, two followers from Emmaus burst into the room and reported that they had been with Jesus, and how they recognized him when he broke bread at their table. While they were still talking about this, Jesus stood among them. The disciples thought they were seeing a ghost! Jesus asked them why they still had doubts, but instead of reprimanding them, he showed them his scars and asked for something to eat, a very unghostly thing to do. Then he taught them, opening their minds, and gave them the mission to witness to all they had seen and heard (Luke 24:36–49).

And, of course, we can add the episode with the twin Doubting Thomas as recorded in the Gospel of John. He did legitimately earn the title, but how did Jesus treat him? He simply said: "Put your finger here; see my hands. Reach out your hand and put it into my side. Stop doubting and believe" (John 20:27). We don't know if Thomas reached out and touched Jesus or not, but we do know that he believed. No doubts!

We add all of this to the ending in Matthew where Jesus met his closest disciples on a mountain in Galilee. Upon seeing him, the disciples "worshiped him; *but some doubted*" (Matt 28:17b). What did Jesus do? He sent them on a mission—no rebukes, no ridicule, no condemnation, no anger, just back to business. Sometimes in the face of sincere doubts, that's all you can do.

WHAT ABOUT US?

What can we draw from Jesus' ongoing encounters with disbelief, even though he was doing exactly what he said he would do, what he was called to do. What can we do when we experience our own forty days and nights of disbelief, when others express doubts about our work, about our plans, about our preparation, or even about who we say we are and what we are called to do? I think it is important to note that Jesus never flew into a defensive rage or ridiculed his doubters. He never called in his lawyers. Rather, he just continued about his business, showing up time after time. He broke bread with his doubters, and he fed them. He was present, letting them come close, feel his wounds, and reach their own conclusions. He blessed them, taught them, healed them, and sent them. He made it evident that he believed in them far more than they believed in him—or in themselves. Honestly, I don't think any of this was easy. I'm sure he felt the stings when those closest to him had their doubts about him, but as he told Pilate shortly before his death, "My kingdom is not of this world" (John 18:36). I think he meant it.

CLOSING COMMENTS

Sadly, the road of disbelief runs both ways. It is part of the human experience, and we are all carriers. It comes when we are unwilling, unable, or unprepared to believe. Since that describes most of us at one time or another, there is good reason to shower other's doubts and disbelief with grace and kindness, even as we hope for the same in our hour of disbelief, and especially so when it lasts forty days and forty nights.

Epilogue

TRYING TIMES TAKE US SOMEWHERE

When I began searching for a book topic that could hold my interest as a writer for eight months or so, I couldn't shake the metaphor of forty days and nights found in the Bible. After all, we all deal with hardships from time to time, whether it be a flood, a failure, a giant, a temptation, a reversal, a major disappointment, or outright despair. What I didn't see coming, however, was just how deeply I would connect with each of the forty days and nights in this book. I salted in some personal stories in several of the chapters, but I could have shared more than one personal story in each chapter. As it turns out, most of us will face a series of hardships during our lifetime—not just one. I realized that that describes my journey to a tee.

I also learned how rewarding and enriching a prolonged study of the Scriptures can be, and how many wonderful resources there are at our disposal if we take the time to enter seriously into conversations that have been going on for centuries. I know for many such a study is understood as unnecessary, dangerous, or even a betrayal to one's faith. For me, it has been a wonderful learning experience. My faith is stronger and deeper now than at any other time in my life.

Finally, the central idea in this book about forty days and nights is that it is a time of hardship and trial, which it is, but it is also a time to transition and hope. Hardships take us somewhere;

they change us. Trying times always do. So often, however, we focus on the hardship or trial and forget that there is a journey to be embraced. We are on our way home, but we focus on the pain of the present rather than on the hope of a new landing place. When that is where we center, we can easily lose our way. We can live with the confidence that while trying times do take us somewhere, God is already there and at work long before we arrive. Thanks be to God!

If I could leave any word with you, the reader, it would be this: life is messy, but God is faithful—all the days of our lives.

www.ingramcontent.com/pod-product-compliance
Lightning Source LLC
Chambersburg PA
CBHW071218160426
43196CB00012B/2340